Pain, Porn and
Complicity

Women Heroes from
Pygmalion to Twilight

Pain, Porn and
Complicity

Women Heroes from
Pygmalion to Twilight

KATHLEEN McCONNELL

WOLSAK
& WYNN

Cover image: *Pygmalion and Galatea* by Etienne-Maurice Falconet,
        Photo©The Walters Art Museum, Baltimore.
Cover design: Rachel Rosen
Cover concept: Ashley Hisson
Book design: Julie McNeill, McNeill Design Arts
Author's photograph: Kathleen McConnell
Typeset in Janson Text
Printed by Ball Media, Brantford, Canada

The publisher gratefully acknowledges the support of the Canada Council for the Arts, the Ontario Arts Council and the Canada Book Fund.

 Canada Council Conseil des Arts
for the Arts du Canada

 ONTARIO ARTS COUNCIL
CONSEIL DES ARTS DE L'ONTARIO

Wolsak and Wynn Publishers Ltd.
280 James Street North
Hamilton, ON
Canada L8R 2L3

 Canadian Patrimoine
Heritage canadien

Library and Archives Canada Cataloguing in Publication

Mac, Kathy, 1961-
        Pain, porn and complicity : women heroes from Pygmalion to Twilight / Kathleen McConnell.

Includes bibliographical references and index.
ISBN 978-1-894987-68-4

        1. Women in popular culture. 2. Women in mass media.
I. Title.

HQ1233.M25 2012   305.42   C2012-907140-4

Printed in Canada on 100% post-consumer recycled content

TABLE OF CONTENTS

INTRODUCTION

"You ask such silly questions.... Nobody knows
what 'real' really means."

– Teddy in Brian Aldiss's short story
"Supertoys Last All Summer Long"

The essays in this volume look at several mass-marketed fictions from contemporary popular culture which feature female protagonists. It does so by contextualizing them amongst manifold other sources – fictions of earlier literary periods, stories from myth, contemporary media and literary theory. Choosing to focus on texts produced for the mass market is itself controversial, in that some influential theorists avow that these are not just examples of, but partake in, the degradation of our increasingly global culture. Jean Baudrillard's 1981 book *Simulacra and Simulation* decries the way that fantasy and reality are distressingly indistinguishable in a culture that accepts Disneyland as authentic (12); he observes "the impossibility of rediscovering an absolute level of the real is of the same order as the impossibility of staging illusion. Illusion is no longer possible, because the real is no longer possible" (19). Theodor W. Adorno and Max Horkheimer's pointed critique of cinema in *Dialectic of Enlightenment* tells a cautionary tale about the ways cultures are corrupted when art is produced in the capitalist cause: "The stunting of the mass-media consumer's powers of imagination and spontaneity does not have to be traced back to any psychological mechanisms; he must ascribe the loss of those attributes to the objective nature of the products themselves, especially to the most characteristic of them, the sound film" (126), and "No independent thinking must be expected from the audience: the product prescribes every reaction" (137).

And yet I am an increasingly unabashed consumer of the very popular culture artifacts Baudrillard, and Adorno and Horkheimer warn will destroy my mind as it destroys our cultures. I'm particularly fond of science fiction and fantasy, genres that depart from realism as radically as writers' stunted imaginations, and studios' and publishers' bloated budgets, can take us.

Thus, I watched or read for my own "pleasure" each of the examples of contemporary popular culture analyzed in this volume before I considered them as objects of study. "Pleasure" is in quotes above because watching and/or reading some of them was not necessarily fun. In fact parts – episodes, seasons and/or entireties in at least one case – inspired me to create a whole new personal category for the worst examples of pop culture: "squirmworthy." But the texts' relative aesthetic worth is immaterial here; the analyses are not reviews and their purpose is not to shape readers' and watchers' tastes. Instead, these essays excavate some of the conceptual substructures of particular mass-marketed fictions, largely in order to consider what those assumptions reveal about our increasingly globalized target-market culture.

Each of the popular culture texts represented here sparked my scholar's mind in some way. In the case of *A.I.: Artificial Intelligence*, the scene in which David cuts off a hank of Monica's hair provides an unexpected echo of the eighteenth century poem "Rape of the Lock." Alternatively, in the case of *Buffy the Vampire Slayer*, the spark was the disproportionate furor that followed the cancelling of two episodes in the wake of the Columbine high school shooting. Irritation at clumsy, conventional campiness of the 2004 *Catwoman* movie provoked my critical treatment, while I found compelling the elegant way *Dark Angel* builds on both the romance of Ovid's myth of "Pygmalion and the Statue" and the tragedy of *Frankenstein*. As for the Twilight Quartet of novels, I simply wanted to understand their baffling, monumental success.

Four of the five mass-marketed texts analyzed here – the television shows *Buffy the Vampire Slayer* and *Dark Angel*, the 2004 movie *Catwoman* and the Twilight quartet of novels – feature female protagonists who have superpowers. Thus, at some point, every essay in this book ponders what happens when a beautiful woman – what Laura Mulvey would call an object of scopophilia, or what the rest of us would more colloquially term "eye candy" – is invested with enough agency to become the central subject.

The only text examined here that does not feature a female superhero protagonist is the movie *A.I.: Artificial Intelligence* which is featured in the first essay because it sets up a useful model for most of the subsequent analysis. *A.I.'s* central relationship is between the hero, a mecha (robot) "boy" called David and the object of its desire, a human woman called Monica. Thus the movie reifies the difficulties in the object-become-subject (David) having sufficient sense of self to understand and then work toward attaining any desire; it also provides a lovely comparison between an object-hero (the robot) and a conventionally objectified beautiful woman. Furthermore, David's desire for Monica conflates parent and beloved in an incest-inflected relationship similar to that in Ovid's myth of "Pygmalion and the Statue," which became a touchstone narrative in the analysis of each popular text represented in this volume.

"Pygmalion and the Statue"

A myth is an archetypal story which remains recognizable despite numerous variations over the centuries. In *The Reception of Myth in English Romanticism* Anthony John Harding observes that "it is the process of transformation and reinterpretation that repays study, not the 'original myth,' which, inevitably, we can only 'know' as a reconstruction" (2). This is certainly true of Ovid's *Metamorphoses*; unable to read it in the original Latin, I have depended largely on John Dryden's eighteenth century verse translation, though I've checked it against William Caxton's fifteenth century, Ted Hughes's twentieth century and David Raeburn's twenty-first century translations.

The fifteen books of Ovid's *Metamorphoses* relate about one hundred forty stories of people and deities, minor and major, transformed: they become animals, birds, trees, waterways, stones…. Of all the stories, though, only in book ten's "Pygmalion and the Statue" does an inanimate object become human. Pygmalion is a sculptor and a misogynist who reviles women in the flesh, though he idolizes Woman in the abstract. While his aversion causes him to withdraw from the social contract – he lives alone, determined never to marry (Dryden lines 2–4) – his veneration causes him to sculpt a statue which embodies all the virtues of good womanhood (lines 7–10, 13–16). The result is so compellingly beautiful to him that he falls in love with it: "He knows 'tis Madness, yet he must adore, / And still the more he knows it, loves the more" (lines 19–20).

Pygmalion begins to act on his desire:

The Flesh, or what so seems, he touches oft,
Which feels so smooth, that he believes it soft.
Fir'd with this Thought, at once he strain'd the Breast,
And on the Lips a burning Kiss impress'd. (lines 21–24)

The sculpture does not return his ardour, so he disengages. But looking at it, again he is caught in the net of his own making; some part of him believes it must be real (lines 25–26). Once more he tries embracing it (lines 27–34), and then, incensed by the lack of response, woos it with gifts of clothing, jewellery and beautiful, expensive accoutrements (lines 35–48). Eventually, he makes a bed for them and "The Solemn Rites perform'd, her calls her Bride" (line 53).

His efforts are in vain. Though visually she is the perfect woman, and though the ivory from which she is sculpted takes on the warmth of the hands that touch it, she cannot respond to his desire. Pygmalion finds this self-sealed situation so distressing that he makes a sacrifice to Venus on her next feast day (line 61), and prays

> Almighty Gods, if all we Mortals want,
> If all we can require, be yours to grant;
> Make this fair Statue mine, he would have said,
> But chang'd his Words for shame; and only pray'd,
> Give me the Likeness of my Iv'ry Maid. (lines 63–67)

Fortunately for Pygmalion, the goddess heard not just his prayer, but also the wish of his heart. Pygmalion rushes home

> And, impudent in Hope, with ardent Eyes
> And beating Breast, by the dear Statue lies.
> He kisses her white Lips, renews the Bliss,
> And looks and thinks they redden at the Kiss:
> He thought them warm before: Nor longer stays,
> But next his Hand on her hard Bosom lays:
> Hard as it was, beginning to relent,
> It seem'd, the Breast beneath his Fingers bent;
> He felt again, his Fingers made a Print,
> 'T was Flesh... (lines 73–82)

Pygmalion renews his lovemaking: "At this the waken'd Image op'd her Eyes, / And view'd at once the Light and Lover, with surprise" (lines 94–95). Unsurprisingly, given Pygmalion's preoccupations and the blessing of the goddess of love, within a year the couple become the parents of a boy named Paphos, who becomes a famous hero and founder of the city of the same name (lines 96–101). Thus the statue's metamorphosis from inanimate object to human woman redeems Pygmalion from solipsistic isolation to become a patriarch of his family and city. The anonymous, animated sculpture's opinion on her fate is not included in Ovid's telling of the myth.

At around a mere hundred lines (depending on the translation), Ovid's "Pygmalion and the Statue" has implications for the contemporary popular texts discussed here, because most of them include a woman's transformation – actual or metaphorical – from object to subject and so invite reflection on the relative agency (or lack thereof) – of the object/subject. Several of them also include relationships that invite discussion of the phenomenon of creator as father and/or lover that Pygmalion evokes.

The Gothic

It is difficult for a text with a female hero to avoid being Gothic, because heroes suffer conflict and betrayal before they succeed (or fail, in the case of tragedies) and, as Michelle A. Massé points out in *In the Name of Love: Women, Masochism and the Gothic*, "the Gothic genre is 'about' suffering women" (1). Certainly a lot of elements associated with the Gothic arise in the popular culture texts analyzed here. Gothic fictions are in essence psychological; in particular, they delve into the ways we perceive the uncanny. According to Freud "the 'uncanny' is that class of the terrifying which looks back to something long known to us, once very familiar" (319–20). By this definition vampires (*Buffy the Vampire Slayer*, *Twilight*); some transgenics (*Dark Angel*) and mechas (*Artificial Intelligence*); even superheroes (Buffy, Catwoman) are uncanny, since they are indistinguishable from humans, yet are not human. Uncanniness leads to uncertainty in the eyes of beholders who cannot trust evidence provided by their senses, and thus uncertainty – according to Fred Botting's book *Gothic* – is central to Gothic texts. The inability to trust our sensory perceptions lead to the larger "uncertainties about the nature of power, law, society, family and sexuality [that] dominate Gothic fiction. They are linked to wider threats of disintegration manifested most forcefully in political revolution" (5); certainly texts like *Dark Angel* and *Buffy the Vampire Slayer* question authority in ways that suggest social insecurity.

In the Gothic fictions of the eighteenth and nineteenth centuries, signature textual attributes included: apparently supernatural phenomena; gloomy, Byronic, mysterious, inscrutable outcast heroes; heroines who are timid and threatened yet persistent and even forceful when necessary; dark, manipulative, evil and ultimately spectacularly self-destructive villains; plots that turn upon long-buried secrets of social and domestic identity, patterns of flight and persecution, ominous threats to the protagonist, and a providential, nigh miraculous design revealed in denouement; exotic, historical settings in labyrinthine dungeons, impenetrable castles, impassable mountains, crumbling ruins; and a lot of pathetic fallacy in which the weather parallels the situation or protagonist's state of mind (Mack xvi–xx). Given that tracking each of these elements through any individual text risks committing what Eugenia C. DeLamotte calls a reductive "shopping list approach" (5; Hoeveler calls it the "Laundry list" [8] approach) to literary criticism of Gothic texts, the analyses provided here are largely limited to those issues earmarked as important by Massé; she considers "formal characteristics of the Gothic – frequently predictable characters, the Ur plot of separation from the known, exposure to horror, alliance of horror and romance plot, and often conservative resolution – as examples of the involuntary repetition Freud associates with the uncanny" (2).

The Essays

The inspiration for "Creating People for Popular Consumption: Echoes of Pygmalion and 'Rape of the Lock' in *A.I.: Artificial Intelligence*" came from the moment in Spielberg's movie when

David, the artificial boy (called a "mecha" in the movie), tries three times before succeeding in shearing a hank of his "mother" Monica's hair. This similarity to Alexander Pope's mock-epic poem "Rape of the Lock" started a train of thought that travelled widely to pick up the elements ultimately needed to discuss *A.I.: Artificial Intelligence*. As a mecha, David is an object that mimics human life and is therefore as uncanny as Pygmalion's statue. This contrasts directly the situation of the real Arabella Fermor whose hair was cut off by the real Robert Lord Petre in 1711, a event that led to the commissioning of Alexander Pope's poem. Arabella Fermor was an aging ingenue; the shearing of her lock had implications of sexual promiscuity which threatened to render her unmarriageable. The essay argues that Pope's poem abrogated any agency in the public sphere Fermor may have had prior to the haircutting incident, a literary act of misuse which the essay shows served the purpose of reinstating Fermor's exchange value in the eighteenth-century marriage market. In *A.I.*, the two situations – the uncanny humanizing of an object and the canny objectification of a human – exist side by side in the relationship of David and Monica. Consequently, though they were produced in widely separate historical periods, these three stories shed light on the social implications of tales about either the humanization of an object or the objectification of a human.

Like "Creating People for Popular Consumption," "Chaos at the Mouth of Hell: *Buffy the Vampire Slayer* and the Columbine High School Massacre" was sparked by an unexpected juxtaposition. I planned on writing a fairly conventional literary analysis exploring Buffy as a role model for third wave feminists, when, in the wake of the Columbine High School shooting, two episodes of the show were cancelled in the US. The disproportionate furor that ensued involved fans, The WB Television Network, the show's producers and performers, the print and television media, politicians at various levels of government, NGOs and the gun lobby. In light of this, my original intention fell by the wayside and I focused instead on untangling the chaotic mix of reactions in order to understand how something as apparently ephemeral as the delayed airing of a quirky television show could achieve public relations parity with something as devastating as the most deadly high school shooting to date in the United States. To do this, the analysis borrows ideas from chaos theory including the "strange attractor," which is the name that theorists give to a phenomenon which they cannot perceive but which has an effect that they can measure. The essay argues that there's a strange attractor at work in high schools in the United States and the perceptible results of its action are school shootings. *Buffy the Vampire Slayer* provides a very cogent metaphor for that strange attractor in the Hellmouth which opens beneath Buffy's school, Sunnydale High.

(I have been working on the Buffy essay for longer than any of the others in this book and research resources have changed drastically since I began. Though scholarship on the show has turned into a virtual industry, in 1999 when first I went to the MLA CD-ROM, and typed in "Buffy" I got nothing. I then tried the Education CD-ROM and was similarly rewarded. So too with Psychology. But when I moved to the Sociology CD-ROM, nine "hits" showed up. "Pay dirt," I thought to myself...and was wrong. Apparently the "Buffy-Headed Marmoset" was a popular experimental animal among some sociologists in the eighties and nineties.)

"Flex and Stretch: The Inevitable Feminist Treatise on *Catwoman*" is probably the most conventional essay included here. It follows the requisite structural sequence for an academic essay: introduction; delineation of the thematic approach; literature review of earlier treatments of the subject, in this case movies which feature the Catwoman; and then the analysis itself, broken into plausible paragraph-equivalent bites; ending in a concluding synthesis of the analysis. Since this "compleat essay" is also in the form of a long poem, it evidences a slight tang of satire on the genre of academic writing. A further effect of the poetic form is that points are not stated as overtly as they would be in a prose essay; the evidence is given in rational order, in the structure as well as the content, but the implications are not always directly drawn. For example, nowhere is it stated that the varied indenting is a way of visually putting a wave into an essay predicated on understanding the three waves of feminism. Including accent marks in the subsection entitled "Ophelia's Exhortatory Sonnet" visually shows that the speeches quoted there – transcribed directly from the film – are largely in iambic blank verse, thereby alluding to the conventionality not only of the character speaking, but also of the film's language, a conventionality that extends to all the aesthetics of the movie, from sets and costumes to camerawork and action sequences.

The second-last subsection, "…And Release," is another transcription, in this instance of Catwoman's voice-over reading the "Dear John" letter to Detective Tom Lone. In the essay, the letter's text has been formed in the shape of an hourglass, an allusion to both a female figure and time's passage; the words explain what the hourglass implies – that life is too short for Catwoman to worry about fitting herself into Lone's pedantic ideas of female virtue (which are, by the way, the same as those embodied by Pygmalion's statue) as constructed and constricting as the catsuit Catwoman wears. The problems with Beau-line, the revolutionary anti-aging cream which figures largely in the plot also evoke details of Ovid's myth – the cream works miraculously, but if you stop using it, you turn to stone.

The final subsection, "Finis," crosses lines of dialogue showing, from left to right, how Patience Phillips and Catwoman eventually come to be integrated in one identity, and from right to left, observations on how the social world portrayed in *Catwoman* has no room for a woman with such an integrated sense of self.

"*Dark Angel*: A Recombinant Pygmalion for the Twenty-First Century" is similar to the first essay in this volume, "Creating People for Popular Consumption," in that the popular text examined in each – *Dark Angel* and *A.I.* – is about the uncanniness of artificially created life; both essays also use a literary precursor to expedite the analysis. However, where "Rape of the Lock" was the unexpected text in the *A.I.* essay, *Dark Angel* provides the opportunity to discuss Mary Shelley's *Frankenstein*, a more obvious precursor as it is in many ways a Gothic retelling of the Pygmalion myth. Neither Pygmalion's statue nor Victor Frankenstein's creature is named in their narratives, suggesting that their creators did not consider them as potentially independent beings; in Pygmalion, this lack of foresight on the part of the creator is immaterial, but all the tragedy in *Frankenstein* stems from that one flaw. Where Pygmalion's statue provides the means for the solipsistic sculptor's social redemption, Victor Frankenstein's creature causes the gregarious scientist's social ostracism. Where Pygmalion and his statue become each other's beloved, Victor Frankenstein and his creature extinguish all hope of love for the other – Victor by destroying the materials that would have become a female creature, and the creature by murdering most of Victor's friends and family, including his wife, Elizabeth Lavenza, on their wedding night.

Pygmalion is both father-creator and lover, and Victor Frankenstein is both father-creator and hater; in *Dark Angel*'s first season that dual role is split between the repressive father-creator Colonel Donald Lydecker who calls her X5-452, and permissive lover Logan Cale, who knows her as Max. The idea of iteration introduced in "Chaos at the Mouth of Hell" is reprised here to discuss how the main character's two names, and the splitting of the father/lover into two roles does not simply result in the dark angel shuttling between one pole to the other, but how her iterated experiences allow her to learn and grow in ways unexplored in Pygmalion and impossible in the gothic plot of entrapment of *Frankenstein*. Finally, since Max's genes include some feline DNA, she is an iteration of Catwoman as evidenced by her preternatural beauty, grace, and ability to jump and climb like a cat – useful skills in her avocation as a cat burglar which she also shares with Catwoman.

"The Twilight Quartet: Romance, Porn, Pain and Complicity" began as a poem similar to "Flex and Stretch." Over many drafts the essay became more complex than I'd anticipated, and the poetic form came to obscure rather than expedite understanding; I began to radically revise it to the prose version provided here. Vestiges of poetry persist in the piece, though, most obviously in the lists – of repetitive quotes concerning Bella Swan's lying in section one, or of the adjectives describing her conflation of Edward's caring and hurting in section three, etc. The poetic genesis of the piece continues covertly in the structure as well; the four sections of the essay are very roughly aligned to the four books of the quartet and model the descent into complicity with Bella Swan's masochism that the books engender in their readers.

The initial plan for the essay on Twilight was to focus on Bella, from whose point of view most of the novels are narrated. However, since the central fantasy of the Twilight books is that of the idolized celebrity boy saving "every-girl Bella Swan from a boring life of domestic chores, distant relationships, and unsatisfying schoolwork" (Aubrey 226), it is nigh impossible to parse Bella without simultaneously discussing her relationship with the vampire Edward Cullen and the other men featured in her narrative: Jacob Black (the wolf shape-shifter) and her father Charlie Swan (strictly human). Furthermore, the Twilight novels' genres – a combination of elements from mass-market romance, pornography and the Gothic, which valorizes masochism – profoundly impact the depiction of Bella and her beaux. Excavating the genre conventions used to frame Twilight's heroine and her heroes goes a long way toward explaining both the quartet's appeal and its perils to uncritical readers.

"First Quarter: Romance" demonstrates ways that Stephenie Meyer's Twilight books use the seemingly innocent elements of the mass-market romances of the 1970s as delineated by Ann Barr Snitow in her essay "Mass Market Romance: Pornography for Women is Different." The "Second Quarter: Porn" analyzes the quartet using the second part of Snitow's analysis, wherein she demonstrates that the relatively inexplicit mass-market romance is actually a kind of diffuse pornography for women, thereby earning the descriptor "abstinence porn" (Seifert). The Twilight quartet of novels mimics the 1970s mass-market romance quite markedly in terms of presenting desire as a matter of delay and repeat.

The "Third Quarter: Pain" is the longest as it analyzes in detail how the quartet's paralleling of sexuality and vampirism equates love with predation, and thereby normalizes heroine Bella Swan's developing desire to be hurt. This section relies heavily on Michelle A. Massé's *In the Name of Love: Women, Masochism, and the Gothic*, which shows ways that the three stages of the beating fantasy (as delineated by Freud and revised by Massé) play out in Gothic novels. The "Fourth Quarter: Complicity" examines how the books present sado-masochism as evidence of romantic love, thereby normalizing masochism amongst its often impressionable readership. The "Complicity" quarter also shows how *Breaking Dawn*, the fourth book in the quartet, becomes an example of the Marital Gothic, in which the husband's attention claustrophobically proscribes the heroine's identity.

The Uncompleted Dream

A book aspires to the illusion of completeness, but writing necessarily involves a concurrent process of ruthless editing. For example, I still worry about whether I should have made room somewhere in the following pages to discuss Lerner and Loewe's musical *My Fair Lady* (itself a revision of George Bernard Shaw's play *Pygmalion*) even though it has no supernatural element. In *My Fair Lady* the created being is an English aristocrat, transformed from the raw material of cockney flower girl Eliza Doolittle. Perhaps some mention could have been slotted into the *Dark Angel* essay, because *My Fair Lady* anticipates *Dark Angel* in that the Pygmalion figure has been split into the repressive father Professor Henry Higgins and the permissive lover Freddy Eynsford-Hill.

If *My Fair Lady* belongs here somehow, then surely its precursor, Maria Edgeworth's 1801 novel *Belinda* does as well. In *Belinda*, Clarence Hervey takes on the Rousseau-inspired project of forming his ward Virginia St. Pierre into the ideal woman, just as Henry Higgins took on Eliza Doolittle; Hervey discovers that, virtuous though she may be, he is not in love with Virginia (Edgeworth 476), and thus provides the literary moment of the splitting of father from lover.

Should W. S. Gilbert's 1871 play *Pygmalion and Galatea* have had a moment in the sun, here? Gilbert's narrative uses the animated statue Galatea's naïveté to explore some of the absurdities of upper class social conventions in Britain, an exploration of some relevance to Buffy from *Buffy the Vampire Slayer*, whose initial naïveté reveals the absurd infantilization of middle American adolescents. (Perhaps I should have found a way to include the information that it wasn't until the Renaissance that the statue's subjectivity was explored sufficiently for her to gain a name for herself – Galatea [Anderson 246], a name hijacked from the lovesick daughter of the sea gods Nereus and Doris, described in *Metamorphoses*' thirteenth book). Gilbert's virtuous Galatea causes so much distress for herself and others that she selflessly chooses to return to stone rather than continue as a source of social upheaval, a transformation that seems reminiscent of Ovid's Propoetides (*Metamorphoses*, book ten), but really is not, since Galatea is a paragon of self-sacrifice – precursor of Twilight's Bella Swan, perhaps? – and the Propoetides are vicious to the core.

Nor is Gilbert's Galatea much like Anaxarete, another Ovidian character who, after some waffling, I decided was not relevant to the following essays. Book fourteen of Ovid's *Metamorphoses* includes the tale of Iphis's abject obsession with stone-hearted Anaxarete, who spurns him; eventually Iphis commits suicide by hanging himself on the door to her house. Anaxarete's remorse is such that she metamorphoses into stone as his funeral procession passes, thereby becoming an enduring monument to his devotion. Surely Twilight's Bella becomes a stony monument to her dead beloved Edward when she becomes a vampire even though she never disdained him as Anaxarete did Iphis – quite the contrary. One could say that *A.I.*'s mecha David embodies both sides of the Anaxarete binary; its fixation on Monica is reminiscent of Iphis's mania for Anaxarete, while its two thousand years of unmoving prayer mimics the monumental Anaxarete.

And what about the rather strange variation on the Pygmalion myth in Shakespeare's play *The Winter's Tale?* In it, King Leontes mourned his perfect wife, Hermione, for sixteen years, dead (he thinks) because of his unfettered and unfounded jealousies. In act five the noblewoman Paulina reveals a statue of Hermione which she then animates through witchcraft, she claims. The play does not explain if the statue is an image of Hermione brought to life, or if Hermione had been turned to stone and is now transformed back to flesh, or if Paulina has been hiding Hermione for the entire sixteen years, and the statue play was a hoax; this ambiguity may have had relevance for *Dark Angel* whose character suffers from prejudicial oppression because her DNA was spliced in a lab rather than a womb, even though there's no obvious outward evidence of her laboratory origins.

Alternatives to the pop culture texts featured here are legion. Summer 2012's Batman movie, *The Dark Knight Rises*, adds yet another generation to the proliferating genealogy of Catwomen; the tragic massacre in Aurora at an opening night showing suggests that the line between illusion and reality has blurred even more than in 1999 when there was a tangential relationship between the Columbine massacre and *Buffy the Vampire Slayer*. E. L. James' wildly popular Fifty Shades trilogy overtly exploits the clandestine sado-masochist economy of the Twilight quartet. Heroines of mass-marketed texts like Merida of *Brave*, or Katniss of Suzanne Collins' *The Hunger Games* continue the trend of female heroes with agency like Buffy and Max Guevara, and provide counters to the way Bella Swan's sense of self is increasingly circumscribed as the Twilight novels progress.

As for theoretical approaches, determining what belonged here and what would tangle the lines of thought kept me up many nights. Should I have included Jeffrey Jerome Cohen's "Monster Culture (Seven Theses)"? Despite their focus on medieval texts, the first two theses – "The Monster's Body is a Cultural Body" (4) and "The Monster Always Escapes" (4) – fits into a discussion of Buffy's encounter with Dracula. And should I have integrated A. C. Goodson's article "Frankenstein in the Age of Prozac" into the discussion of the claustrophobic relationship between creator and creature in the *Dark Angel* essay? Goodson posits that the creature does not exist – the only independent corroboration we have is Walton's observation at the end of the book (Shelley *Frankenstein* 182–85) and he's as monomaniacal as Victor. Victor, suggests Goodson, is profoundly mentally ill, and all the evils that populate his life came from his own madness of which the creature is a symptom (3), thereby further circumscribing the polarity represented by the creature and creator as bipolarity. Should Slavoj Žižek's *Welcome to the Desert of the Real* have had a place in the discussion that opened this introduction? Frankenstein's creature could be seen as a terrorist in Baudrillardian terms; certainly *Dark Angel* invites discussion of activism as terrorism from the point of view of the wealthy retainers of the status quo.

Alas, I reluctantly strangled all these potential lines of enquiry, and more; though they may have been interesting intrinsically, they distract from the main journey of each essay's argument. Instead, the essays here pursue several lines of enquiry in analyzing a mass-marketed science fiction or fantasy text with a traditionally objectified protagonist – female, or artificially created, or both – in the context of the Pygmalion myth and Gothic literature.

1.
CREATING PEOPLE FOR POPULAR CONSUMPTION:

Echoes of Pygmalion and "Rape of the Lock" in *A.I.: Artificial Intelligence*

A.I.: Artificial Intelligence is not a good movie. It *is* a very interesting one, though, because it has a number of what Lesley Stern's article "Paths That Wind through the Thicket of Things" denotes "certain cinematic objects, certain cinematic moments [which] yield more value than others in this quest to understand the Thing" (354). While Stern's quest is limited to objects, this essay explores the way that objects become humanized, and the way that humans become objectified.

Over twenty years in the making, *A.I.: Artificial Intelligence* (commonly called *A.I.*) is based on a short story by Brian Aldiss called "Supertoys Last All Summer Long." That story was optioned by Stanley Kubrick around 1980 and willed to Steven Spielberg who wrote, directed and produced it as a movie (Tibbetts 260). The movie's protagonist, David, is a robot "child" on a quest to become a real boy so his "mother," Monica, a human woman, will love him. The final moments expose one of the movie's key problems, which critic John C. Tibbetts rather coyly frames as a question: "Is the disturbing message here that, in order to love him, she must become something of an artificial life form herself?" (257–58). This query has many implications, and to answer it,

I will take you on a jaunt through some relevant aspects of Bill Brown's "Thing Theory," tour the studio of "Pygmalion" as well as its neighbouring stories in Ovid's *Metamorphoses*, and make an excursion into the socio-historical context of the poem "Rape of the Lock" by Alexander Pope. This winding path provides the ideas necessary to embark upon an analysis of *A.I.* itself.

Despite their generic and temporal diversity, the texts chosen for this essay have in common the subject of the social redemption of an outcast. The basis for the outcast's initial exclusion is different in each. Ovid's tale of "Pygmalion and the Statue" concerns how the solipsistic artist Pygmalion is redeemed to become a valuable member of society; that redemption is mediated through an object rendered uncanny by his treatment of it as if it were human. I use the term "uncanny" here in the sense promulgated by Brown in his 1998 article, "How to Do Things with Things (A Toy Story)." Brown observes that "when the subject-object relation is temporalized to the point of becoming recognizable as a negotiation, when the object appears to assume a life of its own, this is when we discover the uncanniness of everyday life" (939). Brown's essay goes on to complicate Marx's famous binary classification of objects by exchange value and use value through the addition of a "misuse value" category, suggesting "if the use value of an object amounts to its preconceived utility, then its misuse value should be understood as the unforeseeable potential within the object" (956). A misused and misusable object, such as a lifelike statue, has the potential to be treated as if it has cognitive depth, and is therefore inherently uncanny.

"Pygmalion and the Statue"

Though most commonly read as illustrative of the power of the creative imagination, translations of Ovid's "Pygmalion and the Statue" consistently include details that suggest the myth is equally about the sculptor's need for, and achievement of, social redemption. Immediately prior to Pygmalion's story in *Metamorphoses* is that of the Propoetides, women who murdered their guests and were punished by becoming coarse whores. Their moral and spiritual hardness is eventually expressed physically, when they are transformed into flint by Venus, the goddess of love. Consequently, Pygmalion conceives a deep distrust of women and determines never to marry, thereby absenting himself from the human social contract.

To distract himself from his dilemma – caught between disgust and desire – the sculptor takes up his chisel, "And carv'd in iv'ry such a maid, so fair, / As Nature could not with his art compare" (Dryden lines 7–8). As the creator of the statue, he is in the position of a parent to it; despite this, the affection he feels towards the statue is erotic, not paternal. He misuses, in Brown's sense of the term, his creation as if it were a woman. At first, he treats it as a beloved (lines 21–24). Later, he woos it with rich clothes and jewellery (lines 38–42) and even beds his humanized object:

Beauteous she showed, but unadorned the best.
Then from the floor he raised a royal bed,
with coverings of Sidonian purple spread. (lines 42–45)

He knows that this infatuation with his statue is madness (18), and still he loves her. At his wits' end, Pygmalion prays to Venus, the goddess of love:

Make this fair statue mine, he wou'd have said,
But chang'd his words for shame: and only pray'd,
'Give me the likeness of my iv'ry maid.' (lines 65–67)

Impressed by the obsessive love that leads Pygmalion to such excesses of misuse, Venus grants the spirit rather than the letter of his prayer. She endows the statue with life (lines 68–70).

Translations of Ovid's "Pygmalion and the Statue" invariably end with the mention of a son born to him and his sculpture-turned-human:

> The Goddess, present at the match she made,
> So bless'd the bed, such fruitfulness convey'd,
> That ere ten months had sharpen'd either horn,
> To crown their bliss, a lovely boy was born;
> *Paphos* his name, who grown to manhood, wall'd
> The city *Paphos*, from the founder call'd.
> (Dryden lines 96–101)

The son's heroic success caps the father's social redemption, which began with the actual marriage to the statue when it was animated through the intercession of Venus (not the pre-animation mock marriage from the misuse stage of Pygmalion's infatuation).

In the next story in *Metamorphoses*, Ovid goes on to suggest that, though such excesses of desire may be rewarded on the part of father/husband Pygmalion, they are disastrous if felt by the daughter/wife. The story of Myrrha begins with her father Cinyras (himself the son of Paphos; thus Myrrha is Pygmalion's great-granddaughter) asking her which of her many suitors she wants for a husband. She responds with an inversion of Pygmalion's prayer to Venus:

> She felt a secret venom fire her blood,
> And found more pleasure, than a daughter shou'd;
> And, ask'd again, what lover of the crew
> She lik'd the best, she answer'd, One like you.
> Mistaking what she meant, her pious will
> He prais'd, and bid her so continue still:
> The word of Pious heard, she blush'd with shame
> Of secret guilt (Dryden lines 116–23)

Unlike Venus who heard the true desire underneath Pygmalion's misleading words and openly rewarded it, mortal Cinyras hears words of truth but misunderstands the incestuous desire, and therefore encourages it. One dark night, Myrrha seduces her father; their affair carries on until Cinyras discovers that his lover is also his daughter. Appalled, he chases her with a sword, causing her to pray for deliverance. In answer, the gods turn her into a tree. Myrrha's tale ends with the tree's subsequent painful, uncanny travail with Cinyras' child, which is, among other things, a cautionary tale for women who try to hide their illegitimate pregnancies by binding their bellies.

Myrrha's incest results in her social repudiation; just as the Propoetides first became flint-hearted whores and then actual flint, so Myrrha first loses her exchange value as a potential wife, and then is transformed from a human woman into a tree, doomed to suffer childbirth in that rigid form. Clearly, her incestuous desire leads to punishment. On the other hand, Cinyras is characterized as Myrrha's dupe; his transgressions (having sex with his daughter, cheating on his wife) are not at issue.

In Pygmalion's case, what started out as a folly of misuse – Pygmalion's obsessive, incestuous love for the statue he created, which he treats as if it were alive – is the first step toward his redemption.

As for the statue turned into a real woman, Ovid's version neither solicits her opinion about her relationship with her father/husband, nor explores her subjectivity in any manner. Nor does Dryden in his translation of Ovid give any indication of desire on the part of the animated statue. Other translations suggest that she blushed (Raeburn line 293, Hughes line 187, Caxton paragraph 9), an equivocal indicator, perhaps of desire but more likely of modesty; in either case it is the only indication of subjectivity on the part of the uncanny object-become-human.

"Rape of the Lock"

Alexander Pope's "Rape of the Lock" began in 1712 as a two canto poem written to fulfill a private commission to diffuse dissention between two of England's leading Catholic families; by the time of its official publication in 1714, it had grown to become a five canto mock-heroic epic with great public appeal.

Like Ovid's "Pygmalion and the Statue," "Rape of the Lock" is a narrative of social redemption, though with three significant departures from Pygmalion. First, it concerns the reputation of an excessively social woman, Arabella Fermor, who lived in London from 1696 to 1737; unlike Pygmalion, she was neither fictional nor solipsistic. Second, Fermor's redemption is effected through poetry, rather than a mediating object. Third, the ultimate success of the redemption is open to question. Like Pygmalion, Arabella eventually marries, but marriage has the effect of extracting her from society rather than integrating her as it did the sculptor. Furthermore, the poem "Rape of the Lock" characterizes her more as a Propoetide or as Myrrha than as Pygmalion's statue.

Canto one of "Rape of the Lock" begins with a bathetic invocation to the muse, and goes on to describe the ephemeral guardian sylphs of the protagonist, Belinda, who assist as she arms herself for feminine combat, adorning her with makeup and clothing and in particular an elaborate coiffure, including a prominent ringlet by each ear. In canto two, Belinda sallies forth from her dressing room to join the social world; she outshines all her glittering rivals. Canto three sees her downfall, though, as the baron borrows a pair of scissors from Clarissa and cuts off one of Belinda's fore-ringlets. In canto four, Belinda histrionically vents her anger and despair over the assault upon her person by vowing retribution. Canto five brings "war"; the women go to battle against the men, slaying them with frowns or saving them with smiles. Belinda triumphs over the baron, but alas, the lock of hair is lost – the poet suggests it has been bodily assumed into heaven, being too perfect for this fallen world.

Understanding the serious situation which underlies this sustained, frothy narrative requires an appreciation of the situation of Catholics in the England of 1714; at that time, landed Roman Catholics like the Fermors had to pay double-taxes which seriously depleted their wealth (Rumbold 66) and thus diminished the resources available for their daughters' dowries. However, marriage to Catholics in the professions was considered beneath these aristocratic families, despite its potential as an avenue for avoiding financial ruin. For example, when Michael Blount, the heir of the Blount family, was betrothed to Mary Eugenia Strickland, who was the daughter of a wealthy lawyer, Michael's sister Teresa Blount, wrote that "to have such odd folks dare to think of him; is to great a humiliation I shal Laugh em to scorn in al Companys [sic]" (63). Despite Teresa's disapproval, Michael married Mary Eugenia. Marriage to non-Catholic aristocrats was even less likely, as the division between Catholic and Protestant was very strictly regarded in the eighteenth century. As a result, the pool of appropriate spouses for women like Arabella Fermor, and Pope's friends Patty and Teresa Blount, was very small; Rumbold attests that, though famous, successful and Catholic, Alexander Pope himself would have been beneath the Blounts, since the poet had no significant real estate to his name (52).

In the poem "To a Young Lady, With the Works of Voiture," Pope details the ways in which the marriage market defines and limits unmarried women:

Too much *your Sex* is by their Forms confin'd,
Severe to all, but most to Womankind;
Custom, grown blind with Age, must be your Guide
Your Pleasure is a Vice, but not your Pride;
By nature yielding, stubborn but for Fame;

> Made Slaves by Honour, and made Fools by Shame. (lines
> 31–36)

The poem goes on to show how even a good match can lead to an unhappy life:

> The Gods, to curse *Pamela* with her Pray'rs,
> Gave the gilt Coach and dappled *Flanders* Mares,
> The shining Robes, rich Jewels, Beds of State,
> And to compleat her Bliss, a Fool for Mate.
> She glares in *Balls*, *Front-boxes*, and the Ring,
> A vain, unquiet, glitt'ring, wretched Thing! (lines 49–54)

Despite his sympathy, the conservative Pope gives no indication of wanting to change the social status quo. He merely grieves that men do not fulfill their social obligations to the women who are necessarily dependent on them.

On the other hand, the expense of supporting unattached women in a style appropriate to their social status could easily become a considerable burden on a family's finances. In fact, for nearly forty years after Michael Blount's death, his widow Mary Eugenia drew a jointure (a provision for a wife after her husband's death) from Michael's family, which severely limited the resources available for the dowries of her own granddaughters (Rumbold 66). Inadequate dowries put women of marriageable age in a very difficult position: it wasn't enough to be beautiful or have the right family connections, or even to be witty. One had to have money to marry one's social equal, and Roman Catholic wealth was being severely attenuated through taxes and social obligations. When the father of Teresa and Patty Blount died in 1710, his estate was not sufficient to meet the obligations stipulated in his will. The sisters were left with insufficient dowries, and so did not have what they considered appropriate suitors. Teresa's case renders the paramount importance of wealth particularly clear: she was socially adept, popular, beautiful and witty. But she was not rich enough – did not have sufficient exchange value – to receive an offer equal to her expectations, and so she did not marry (Rumbold 60).

In this heightened atmosphere of marriage-market tension, the wealthy and eligible Robert Lord Petre committed his famous assault upon the less well-off family friend Arabella Fermor. There is no exact record of the incident that led to the request of Pope's friend and patron John Caryll for a poem to heal a rift that concerned three of the great landed Roman Catholic families in England – the Fermors, the Petres and the Carylls. What is known is that at a party in 1711, Lord Petre snuck up behind Arabella Fermor and cut off a lock of her hair (Tillotson 82), an act with salacious overtones of implied intimacy. Pope describes his commission as follows:

> The stealing of Miss Belle Fermor's hair, was taken too seriously, and caused an estrangement between the two families, though they had lived so long in great friendship before. A common acquaintance and well-wisher to both, desired me to write a poem to make a jest of it, and laugh them together again. It was with this view that I wrote the Rape of the Lock. (Quoted in Tillotson 81; Tillotson gives evidence that the "well-wisher" was John Caryll, the former guardian of Robert Lord Petre.)

Tellingly, Robert Lord Petre – the scissor-wielding baron of "The Rape of the Lock" – married Catherine Walmsley before the first edition of the poem was published in 1712. Walmsley was several years younger than Arabella Fermor and brought a dowry that was worth at least double that of Fermor (Tillotson 92). Thus, Lord Petre's impending marriage to someone else seemed to indicate that, while Arabella Fermor was playing the marriage game in earnest in 1711, Lord Petre was just playing when he cut off her ringlet.

Although probably acquainted with Arabella Fermor, Pope was far more familiar with Teresa Blount, and there is some critical speculation that he wrote "Rape of the Lock" with both women in mind, though the evidence is fairly tenuous; throughout the poem, Pope uses non-specific terms like "bright," "glittering" and "fair" for "Belinda's" tresses. The one exception is line 169 of Canto IV, which states "These in two *sable* Ringlets…" (italics added). Though the fictional Belinda of the poem is ostensibly Arabella Fermor, she had light brown hair; Teresa Blount's hair was black. There's no record of an incident in Blount's life similar to the rape of Arabella Fermor's lock of hair; nevertheless, in 1714 both Fermor and Blount were in their mid-twenties, which was old for the marriage market. Both were educated at the same convent school in Paris (Rumbold 67), but they seem to have been far from equally literate. As far as contemporary scholarship can tell, Arabella Fermor has left no examples of her own writing to history; she is wholly defined by others' words. Further, Arabella did not fully comprehend the sexual innuendoes in the "Rape of the Lock" until they were pointed out to her after publication. In contrast, these allusions would have been quite clear to Teresa, who carried on a lively correspondence with a number of friends, including Pope, in a mock-gallant style, rife with indecent double entendre (Rumbold 50–53).

Though she didn't write, Arabella delighted in being the subject of writing. She was so pleased with the "Rape of the Lock" when it was first delivered to her that she is generally blamed for the number of unofficial copies in circulation, which Pope claimed as the reason that his authoritative version needed to be published. When the expanded version of the poem was prepared in 1714 (after she had been apprised of the poem's scandalous possibilities), Pope offered Arabella the choice between a dedication which named her and a preface which did not. She preferred to see her name in print:

As to the Rape of the Lock, I believe I have managed the dedication so nicely that it can neither hurt the lady nor the author. I writ it very lately, and upon great deliberation; the young lady approves of it…. A preface which salved the lady's honour, without affixing her name, was also prepared, but by herself superceded in favour of the dedication. (Pope quoted in Tillotson 93)

Furthermore, her niece recalls that "Mr. Pope's praise made her aunt very troublesome and conceited" (quoted in Rumbold 79). Since virtuous women aspired to a retired domesticity, Arabella's enjoyment of her fame implies that she was less than perfectly virtuous.

The "Rape of the Lock" casts further aspersions on Arabella's character and chastity; Canto V characterizes "Belinda" (the fictional Arabella – both names contract to "Belle") as a shrill "virago" (line 37), inciting mock battle over the return of her lock. Her anguished cry at the end of Canto IV – "Oh hadst thou, Cruel! been content to seize / Hairs less in sight, or any Hairs but these" (lines 175–76) – implies that Lord Petre had access to those "hairs less in sight." Furthermore, the reason that Belinda's guardian spirit, Ariel, can no longer protect the maid is that, at the moment of her greatest danger, Belinda thinks upon an earthly lover:

Just in that instant, anxious Ariel sought
The close Recesses of the Virgin's Thought;
As on the Nosegay in her Breast reclin'd,
He watch'd th' Ideas rising in her Mind,
Sudden he view'd, in spite of all her Art,
An Earthly Lover lurking at her Heart.
Amaz'd, confus'd, he found his Pow'r expir'd,
Resign'd to Fate, and with a Sigh retir'd. (canto III lines 139–46)

In the heightened atmosphere of the marriage market, the marginally impure thoughts of Belinda are responsible for her downfall, and the baron is only an agent of that doom (though the efficacy of Belinda's guardian sylphs is dubious even prior to her prurient musing; the sylphs are bathetic versions of the gods of the *Iliad* whose effect in the war between the Trojans and the Achaeans continues to be debated). This is in direct contrast with Pygmalion's successful prayer to Venus – the goddess reads and bestows the wish of the sculptor's heart; Belinda, like Myrrha, is vanquished because of the wish of her heart, though in Belinda's case that wish could not be more attenuated. Still, by admitting any passion, however privately, Belinda exceeds the limits of appropriate agency for an object of exchange on the marriage market.

Just as Pygmalion created the statue, Pope created Belinda and thereby cannily satirized the provocative chastity required of marriageable women, in a manner that a reader like Teresa Blount would appreciate. In the third canto of "Rape of the Lock," the baron makes his play to cut off Belinda's ringlet; three times the baron approaches, and three times Belinda looks around, prompted by her guardian sylphs (canto III lines 137). Just prior to the fourth time, she thinks of her earthly lover, as described in the passage quoted above; this ephemeral evidence of impurity necessitates that her sylphs retire from the field. Unprompted by them, Belinda keeps her head bent and the baron succeeds in severing her lock of hair (canto III lines 153–54).

The weapon which severs Belinda's lock is a pair of scissors; by describing scissors as "a two edged weapon" (canto III lines 128), Pope connotatively allies them with an epic hero's sword, a phallic weapon sharpened on its two outside edges and appropriate for bringing down a male warrior. Conversely, the two edges of a pair of scissors are internal and come into play only when the scissors are opened to provide an appropriately female space, as Pope points out in the lines: "The Peer now spreads the glitt'ring Forfex wide, / T' inclose the Lock; now joins it to divide" (canto III lines 147–48). A pair of scissors, then, is an appropriate machine for vanquishing a woman, which also suggests why it is the lady

Clarissa who, squire-like, supplies Lord Petre with his weapon (canto III lines 137–40). Furthermore, scissors have many of the satirizable attributes of a coquette on the marriage market; both are characterized as rounded on the outside, edged internally around an absence. (This is meant figuratively, of course, in reference to the edged wittiness of women otherwise bereft of intelligent conversation.) As well, ingenues must work hard to attract, without seeming to do so – a perversity suggestive of the scissors' opening to enclose and joining to divide.

Where Pygmalion's chisel creates the statue, Pope uses a real pen and fictional scissors to "make" Arabella Fermor. "Rape of the Lock" was commissioned ostensibly to heal a rift between families, but also to get Arabella back into a more conventional social situation; her 1714 marriage to Mr. Francis Perkins supplies the most persuasive proof that the poem succeeded in this specific aim. Interestingly, two letters Pope wrote upon hearing of Arabella's marriage suggest that the aspersions about her reputation were grounded in substantial rumour, if not fact. To the bride, he sent polished and polite congratulations, though with implications he seemed confident she would miss:

> You are by this time satisfy'd how much the tenderness of one man of merit is to be prefer'd to the addresses of a thousand. And by this time, the Gentleman you have made choice of is sensible, how great is the joy of having all those charms and good qualities which have pleas'd so many, now apply'd to please one only....
>
> It may be expected perhaps, that one who has the title of Poet, should say something more polite on this occasion: But I am really more a well-wisher to your felicity, than a celebrater of your beauty. Besides, you are now a married woman, and in a way to be a great many better things than a fine lady; such as an excellent wife, a faithful friend, a tender

parent, and at last as the consequence of them all, a saint in heaven.... (Tillotson 101)

By marrying, Arabella appears to abandon her erstwhile, inappropriate celebrity as someone who has "pleas'd so many" and aspire to the virtues embodied by Pygmalion's mute, retiring statue.

Pope sent a much more pointed assessment of Arabella's match to Teresa Blount:

> It was but tother day I heard of Mrs Fermor's being Actually, directly, and consummatively, married. I wonder how the guilty Couple and their Accessories at Whiteknights look, stare, or simper, since that grand Secret came out which they so well concealed before. They conceald [*sic*] it as well as a Barber does his Utensils when he goes to trim upon a Sunday and his Towels hang out all the way: Or as well as a Fryer concealed a little Wench, whom he was carrying under his habit to Mr. Colingwood's Convent; Pray Father (sayd one in the Street to him) what's that under your Arm. A Saddle for one of the Brothers to ride with, quoth the Fryer. Then Father (cryd he) take care and shorten the Stirrups – For the Girls Legs hung out –. (quoted in Rumbold 79)

Anyone reading this passage cannot help but wonder at the nature of the "grand secret." Was Arabella's imperfect virtue merely a matter of casual slander between Pope and Blount, or did Fermor have a grand, pregnant belly corseted to her trunk, like the metamorphosed Myrrha? In either case, Pope's canny characterization of Arabella as Belinda misuses her as exploitatively as Pygmalion misused his statue, by subjecting her to the very innuendo he satirizes with observations like "At ev'ry Word, a Reputation dies" (canto III lines 16). Despite the scandalous connotations, Pope's poem is successful on a public, pragmatic level, in that it reinstated Arabella Fermor's exchange value in the marriage market.

In the end, Pope's putatively redemptive caricature Belinda portrays Arabella Fermor not as a modest and virtuous woman like the animated statue, but as a Propoetide wannabe – a putative whore available for objectification. Where Pygmalion achieves social integration through interaction with his creation, Arabella's identification with Pope's creation extracted her from an inappropriate social celebrity and cloistered her in marriage. Three centuries later, synecdoche and the selective artifacts of history retain knowledge of the poem and poet but little of the woman; Arabella Fermor is reduced to Belle and reified into an uncanny tress.

A.I.: Artificial Intelligence

A.I.: Artificial Intelligence takes place in a dystopian future in which a company called Cybertonics is developing a line of child "mechas" (mechanical humans, or robots). They become virtually indistinguishable from real children through a process called imprinting, which is a programmed replication of the parent-child bond of love. One of the first mecha children is tested out in the Swinton family, whose biological child, Martin (Jake Thomas), is in stasis because of an incurable disease. Initially hostile toward what she sees as a poor substitute for Martin, Monica Swinton (Frances O'Connor) gradually becomes more accustomed to the mecha David (Haley Joel Osment), eventually warming enough to initiate the imprinting process that will cause it to simulate reactions to her as if it were her child. She even gives Martin's robotic toy bear – named Teddy – to David. Inevitably, a cure is found for Martin who returns to find a rival in David. Martin becomes increasingly cruel toward the mecha, until Henry Swinton (Sam Robards) insists that it be returned to Cybertonics for disassembly. Unwilling to collude in the "death" of her mecha child, Monica instead abandons him and Teddy in the woods.

With the literalness of a child, David decides to find the Blue Fairy so he can become a real boy that Monica will love. After numerous adventures, David and Teddy find a statue of the Blue Fairy in a *Pinocchio*-themed section in the ruins of Coney Island. Two thousand years pass; human die out; ice locks David, Teddy and the statue of the Blue Fairy in stasis; and still David prays to be made into a real boy. Eventually, members of a race of super-mechas find David and Teddy. They reluctantly agree to clone Monica from cells in the tress of hair that David cut off, even though such clones live only one day. The clone, mecha and supertoy pass an idyllic day together, at the end of which the Monica clone tells David she loves him and David finally sleeps.

David, the prototype mecha child, is programmed to show "love" for the object of its programming, in his case Monica. She is a futuristic June Cleaver, who doesn't know how to define herself without a child. In "The Dreamlife of Androids" J. Hoberman describes the *A.I.* milieu as a "vaguely established, remarkably homogenous, bizarrely suburban, post-greenhouse-effect world of strict family planning and robot sex slaves" (17). The fashions of *A.I.* are inescapably reminiscent of a 1950s vision of the future, an appropriate alignment according to Bill Brown, who observes that the 1950s were a decade when objects like mass-produced Charlie McCarthy and Shirley Temple dolls "defamiliarize[d] the object into a thing that can attain a new kind of presence" (940); Brown's article discusses how the dolls invite the kind of misuse – negotiation with them as if they had agency – that implies they are uncanny. Defamiliarized "into a new presence" certainly describes the mecha David by the end of *A.I.* Dowered with the reactions of a human boy – or rather, programmed to simulate human responses to specific stimuli – David's success is measured by the compassionate responses it excites from the people with whom it interacts, especially the permanently confused Monica. Furthermore, by evoking an era immediately prior to popular social movements like women's liberation, civil rights and anti-war, the social world of *A.I.* rests on a model reminiscent of "Rape of the Lock," whose publication predated the social upheaval of the late-eighteenth and early-nineteenth centuries' industrial revolution in Britain.

A.I. is based on the 1969 short story "Supertoys Last All Summer Long" by Brian Aldiss and aspects of the original short story remain integral to the movie. For example, at the end of its mere two thousand words, the mechanical boy says to its supertoy, "Teddy – I suppose Mummy and Daddy are real, aren't they?" to which Teddy answers, "You ask such silly questions, David. Nobody knows what 'real' really means" (paragraphs 114–15). Certainly, the humanity of the movie's mechanical boy is questioned and answered by this statement; since nobody knows what "real" means, in the end David is as real as real can be.

But David's question also reflects on the possible unreality of the objectified mother in both story and movie. In "Supertoys" she is described as

> Monica Swinton, twenty-nine, of graceful shape and lambent eye, [sitting] in her living room, arranging her limbs with taste. She began by sitting and thinking; soon she was just sitting. Time waited on her shoulder with the maniac sloth it reserves for children, the insane, and wives whose husbands are away improving the world. (paragraph 9)

Aldiss's conservative characterization of Monica is part of a critical examination of the social dynamic of the privileged nuclear family. Not long after the description quoted above, Aldiss reveals the patriarchal structure of the Swinton family:

> Henry Swinton, Managing Director of Synthank, was about to make a speech.
>
> "I'm sorry your wife couldn't be with us to hear you," his neighbor said.

"Monica prefers to stay at home thinking beautiful thoughts," said Swinton, maintaining a smile.

"One would expect such a beautiful woman to have beautiful thoughts," said the neighbor.

Take your mind off my wife, you bastard, thought Swinton, still smiling. (paragraph 11–15)

Thus, the designation "supertoy" applies to most of the characters in the text; just as Teddy is David's supertoy, and David is a supertoy for Monica, so Monica herself is a supertoy for her husband, Henry. Aldiss critiques the claustrophobic role of the trophy wife by situating Monica within a hierarchy of artificial beings. This is not to say that Aldiss promulgates a revolution in women's roles; in the end of the short story, Monica is redeemed from artificiality, not through an assertion of independence, but through the legal sanction of her desire to have a real child.

Aldiss's conservative characterization of Monica underwent decades of editorial tinkering to surface in the movie without the critique; in one early scene, Monica reads *Freud on Women: A Reader*, affirming her characterization as someone who defines herself within the conservative parameters Freud reiterated for women: daughters, wives, mothers. The movie's Monica is rudderless and impulsive, first because she has no child, and then because she has one too many. Truly, Monica searches desperately for a monolithic raison d'être like the programming that motivates David.

In the beginning of its time as part of the Swinton's household, David fits into Brown's definition of an uncanny object which "appears to assume a life of its own" (939), and as such, Monica is constantly spooked by it. Once David has been imprinted with Monica as its "Mummy" – a procedure that she initiates – it has a raison d'être; it exists solely to fulfill Monica's need for a child. Thus far it is used as expected, even though ominous Freudian overtones begin to amass with such startling rapidity that critics seemed unable to resist the "o" word: Oedipal (see Hoberman 17 and Tibbetts 261).

When Monica's biological child, Martin, returns from cryogenic suspension, David becomes truly extraneous and subject to misuse.

Martin initially assumes that David is a toy for himself; when he realizes that David is for his mother, and is therefore competition, Martin encourages David into inappropriate behaviours, first by eating spinach which gums up its mechanical parts. Next, Martin persuades David that it must cut Monica's hair while she is sleeping. (David has been programmed to take initiative in order to satisfy his obsession, and is therefore vulnerable to Martin's manipulation.) As in "Rape of the Lock," David makes three tries for a lock of Monica's hair: she moves in her sleep, and wakes with one blade of the scissors almost in her eye just as it snips. Much hysteria ensues, as in the equivalent scene in Pope's "Rape of the Lock." But David is not finally banished from the household until it endangers Monica's biological son; while at a birthday party, David grabs on to Martin for protection from a bully and they fall into the pool – it looks like the mecha is trying to drown the human. At this point, the patriarch of the Swintons decrees that David must go back to the factory, which leads to Monica irresponsibly releasing it into the wild, as if it is an unwanted kitten.

The balance of the movie is taken up with David's quest to find and petition the Blue Fairy of *Pinocchio* fame to turn him into a real boy deserving of Monica's undivided attention. (It was Martin who insisted that Monica read *Pinocchio* at bedtime, and so planted this idea in David's mind [Hoberman 17].) David's desire is eventually fulfilled – through the creation of an artificial Monica, and not by David's transformation into a human. The members of the race of super-mechas which evolved during David's two thousand years of prayer agree to clone Monica using cells from the lock of hair which was partly responsible for David's initial expulsion from Monica's society, even though, as they explain to David, a clone can only live for one day.

As in the other two narratives examined here, the outcast prays. Pygmalion's prayer in the temple of Venus was of human duration, and his coy substitution of a plausible request – a maid *like* his statue – for his real desire is appropriate to a man unconsciously seeking social redemption; it results in the animation of the misused statue who bears his hero-child Paphos. Belinda's ephemeral thought of a sweetheart befits her token subjectivity, and is central to the chain of narrative events which reinstate Arabella into her marriage-market niche. David's two-millennium mantra underscores both its mechanical constitution and, more ominously, the strength of its programmed obsession with Monica. Like Pygmalion, David's prayer is answered in spirit rather than in actuality, indicating that the disturbing answer to Tibbetts' question of whether or not Monica must become artificial to be loved is a clear "yes."

In the most blatant of the many narrative weaknesses of *A.I.*, the super-mechas regret that a Monica clone can live for only one day; that is enough for David. At the end of its perfect day of games with Monica and Teddy, in bed with the Monica clone, David finally closes its eyes and the voice-over narrates, "For the first time in his life, David went to that place where dreams are born." Given the family romance that the scene inevitably evokes, the voice-over and closed eyes allude to a post-coital loss of consciousness. It further implies that, for David as for the Monica clone, such a loss of consciousness means death. Brown calls this misuse value "part of an uncompleted dream" (956); David's uncanny dream of inclusion is completed by the fusion with Monica that their perfect day together represents.

A.I. conflates and transforms the sexual and marital connotations of "Rape of the Lock" with the incestuous connotations of the Pygmalion and Myrrha myths. Just as the object of Pygmalion's desire is his creation, and therefore his daughter as well as wife, so David's desire causes the creation of the Monica clone, who is thus daughter in the Pygmalion sense, mother according to his programming, and, by the end of the perfect day, virtual wife. Furthermore, because it is the masculine side of the heterosexual binary that expresses incestuous desire in *A.I.*, its fulfillment is depicted as a positive comfort, like the desire of Pygmalion, rather than that of Myrrha.

Over the course of the movie, David moves from being an object prized for use value – a replacement child in the childless Swinton household – to one subject to constant misuse, because its quest to find the Blue Fairy subjects it to adventures unanticipated by its programming. As Brown predicts of misused objects, David develops agency through misuse, first by Martin then by Monica who contravenes her contract with his manufacturer by releasing David into the wild rather than returning him to the factory. From that point on, he is entirely outside of his use-value milieu: every further experience constitutes misuse, and leads to learning. He encounters his private Pygmalion, programmer Professor Hobby, who is delighted with the initiative his creation has shown, not understanding the depth of David's obsession.

By the movie's end, David has more agency than the ephemeral Monica; the boy dreams, but the woman's clone dies. This transfer of subjectivity is underscored by the camerawork. For example, in the beginning of the movie, there are shots of Monica making coffee, while David stares at the mug; in the end the roles are reversed and we see David making coffee, while the Monica clone stares at the mug. When the Monica clone drifts into death at the end of the perfect day, it says to David, "I love you more than anything in the world." So, in contrast to Venus's response to the spirit rather than the letter of Pygmalion's prayer for a maid "like" his statue – the living man's obsession is brought to life – David's two-thousand-year prayer to become a real boy is answered not literally by its transformation but in spirit by the creation of an ersatz Monica. This is reminiscent of the way that Pope's Belinda, an ersatz Arabella, leads to Arabella's restoration as an appropriate exchange object in the marriage market.

Monica is denied even that marginal agency. The movie's Monica is glossily made over, but at the core she is as ominously and purposely empty as Aldiss's original, of whom the short story's David observes: "Her face was blank: its lack of expression scared him. He watched fascinated. He did not move: she did not move" (paragraph 67). The human woman is blank: the mechanical boy is scared. Furthermore, David achieves redemption through the abstraction of Monica from husband, family and community, to concentrate wholly on him. David has become her Pygmalion, and she, an absence subject to the desire of her creator. There is no redemption for Monica: not as an uncanny object, and certainly not as subject. Finally, where Pygmalion's statue's subjectivity simply gets no mention in Ovid's narrative, Monica's subjectivity is revoked. The human becomes an object that doesn't need redemption. On the other hand, David, the uncanny, humanized object is redeemed from the wilderness by its obsession, accepted into a mecha society and given its heart's desire. Thus, the relationship between David and Monica in *A.I.* combines the trope of the uncanny object misused into humanity of Ovid's "Pygmalion and the Statue" with that of a human cannily misused as an object as exemplified by Belle in Pope's "Rape of the Lock."

The largely silent presence behind the discussion in this essay has been, in many ways, Papa Freud, who is the subject of the book which Monica reads; the theorizer of the Oedipal family romance in which the male child wants to replace the father in the mother's affection, as does David with Monica; and the explorer of the uncanniness which informs both the objectification of Belinda/Arabella and the incestuous love of Pygmalion for his daughter/object. Bill Brown's object theory, too, gestures toward Freud. Brown completes the statement about misuse value quoted at the beginning of this essay by further refining his appreciation of the uncanny object's potential as part of the dream work:

> If the use value of an object amounts to its preconceived
> utility, then its misuse value should be understood as
> the unforeseeable potential within the object, part of an
> uncompleted dream....
>
> Such potential is indistinguishable from the hope of
> overcoming the oppression of everyday life, which is no more

sociological or ideological than it is iconological, experienced as the pressure of a culture's dominant images. (956)

Though the three narratives discussed here explore the potential of objects to develop selfhood, they do so without questioning assumptions about the everyday, oppressive objectification of the feminine, arguably one of contemporary western culture's "dominant images." Certainly contemporary advances in reproductive technologies and cloning add a sense of timeliness to narratives about "made" beings, like Ovid's Pygmalion, which explores not only the art object's uncanniness but also the artist subject's redemption through the misuse of an object. In contrast, Pope used literature to turn Arabella from a socially unknowable "virago" (Pope canto V lines 37) into something more familiar – a female object, properly available for marriage, apparently cured of her uncanny tendency to express unsanctioned desires.

Those strategies coexist in the very misuse that demonstrates David's uncanny humanity, which comes at the cost of Monica's subjectivity. There's something deeply disturbing about a manufactured object achieving self-fulfillment through the objectification of a human subject, particularly when the former is gendered male, the latter female. "Pygmalion and the Statue" and *A.I.* reiterate the dangerous message that obsessive love is, for males, a path toward independent subjectivity and social redemption. In addition, according to the same texts and "Rape of the Lock," the highest function of a good woman is not to develop independent subjectivity within a social context, but to become the object of obsessive, even incestuous desire, and thereby a male's means of redemption. Consequently, examination of *A.I.* in the light of Ovid's "Pygmalion and the Statue" and Pope's "Rape of the Lock" demonstrates that the premise driving the movie's plot forward is that social redemption is far more plausible if you are an uncanny object that mimics masculinity than if you're a woman.

2.
CHAOS AT THE MOUTH OF HELL:

Buffy the Vampire Slayer
and the Columbine High School Massacre

In the pilot episode of *Buffy the Vampire Slayer* (aired on March 10, 1997), Buffy's watcher tells her, "Into each generation a Slayer is born, one girl in all the world, a Chosen One, one born with the strength and skill to hunt the vampires –" Then he asks: "What do you know about this town?" to which Buffy replies, "It's two hours on the freeway from Neiman Marcus?" Clearly, Buffy would rather be shopping for shoes than fighting massed evil. A lot of the show's humour lies in dropping a gothic fate onto a valley girl, resulting in a mix aptly described as *Batman* meets *Clueless*.

From 1997 to 2003, fans watched Buffy Summers (Sarah Michelle Gellar) fight evil in suburban Sunnydale, the small California town whence she and her mother Joyce (Kristine Sutherland) moved after Buffy burnt down her previous high school's gym in Los Angeles; the principal was unimpressed by her claim that it was infested with vampires at the time. Alas, the move to Sunnydale doesn't help wean Buffy from what her mother considers inappropriate violence. The should-be innocuous town hosts a horde of monsters – most populous of which are vampires – because it is built on a spot where the barrier between earth and the demon dimensions thins out, creating something called the

Hellmouth. Demons issue forth from, and humans with demonic intentions are mystically attracted to, the Hellmouth and its most fragile point happens to be just beneath the library of Buffy's new school.

Buffy doesn't fight alone; the school librarian, an Englishman named Rupert Giles (Anthony Stewart Head), represents an organization called the Watcher's Council which has records of all the slayers and their watchers over the centuries. Buffy's friends also help out. The core group includes everyman Xander Harris (Nicholas Brendon) and Willow Rosenberg (Alyson Hannigan), who eventually develops into a powerful witch; over the seasons, others come and go from the Scooby Gang, as they call themselves.

Along with episodic plots, each season has a villain whose defeat increases in difficulty as Buffy grows as a slayer and as a person. Season one's "Master" is a powerful Nosferatu-type vampire who manages only to kill Buffy physically. She is revived by Xander and goes on to "dust" the Master. (In *Buffy the Vampire Slayer*, vampires explode into dust when slain.) The Master is topped in season two by the evil incarnation of Buffy's boyfriend, Angel (David Boreanaz), the only good vampire in the world...most of the time. When Buffy dies at the end of season one, another slayer is called, which made it possible in season three for Buffy to square off with a corrupt version of herself, in the person of another slayer. In season four, Buffy again faces a version of herself but augmented; Adam is a conscienceless, Frankensteinian construct made up of demon parts. Season five's villain exceeds the vampire/slayer/demon paradigm; Glory is a god who threatens Buffy's family. Even worse for Buffy, season six's chief villain turns out to be her best friend Willow. Finally, in season seven, Buffy struggles ostensibly against the nameless First Evil, though the actual struggle is to find a way to help people save themselves, which is the only way for her to escape her ordained fate.

When the idea of writing on *Buffy the Vampire Slayer* first formed in my mind in 1999, I intended to explore ways in which the show appeared to deal with crises central to personality development in adolescents, particularly girls. To their credit, writers followed the lead of creator and producer Joss Whedon in portraying

> date rape ('The Pack,' 1:6), domestic violence ('I Only Have Eyes for You,' 2:19; 'Ted,' 2:11; 'Beauty and the Beasts,' 3:4), street kids and homelessness ('Anne,' 2:1), crippling parental/ adult pressure and expectations ('The Witch,' 1:3; 'Go Fish,' 2:20; 'Nightmares,' 1:10), childhood illness, death and trauma ('Killed by Death,' 2:18), (drug) addiction ('Wrecked,' 6:10) and family break-up ('Nightmares,' 1:10)...parental terminal illness or death...('The Body,' 5:13). (Bloustien 438. NB: Bloustien's list extends only as far as the fifth season)

Despite these progressive topics, the social milieu felt conservative to me; a quick look at the show's main characters in the high school years – blond Buffy; her undead, once-Irish love interest Angel; her watcher, the terribly English Rupert Giles; and her schoolmates Xander, Cordelia, Willow and Oz – shows no significant cultural diversity, and nary a zit to be seen either. Though most episodes explored a relevant issue, they began and ended in a relatively affluent, middle-class world. The contrast between the edgy subject matters and conventional social realm led me to posit that *Buffy the Vampire Slayer* belongs in the genre of the Gothic. In her book *In the Name of Love*, Michelle A. Massé notes that an "often conservative resolution" is one of the "formal characteristics of the Gothic" (2). Thus, my initial intention was to stay within the fictions presented in specific episodes of *Buffy the Vampire Slayer* and provide an analysis of popular narrative as a cultural mirror. I planned to show the inherent conservatism of the show's presentation of middle-class female students' struggles to grow up, struggles symbolized by

Buffy's fights against the monsters who rose from the Hellmouth weekly.

My essay changed drastically when, at 11:10 a.m. on April 20, 1999, Eric Harris and Dylan Klebold entered Columbine High School in Littleton, Colorado, each armed with a sawed-off shotgun and a handgun. By 12:08 p.m., twenty-four people were injured and fifteen more were dead, including Harris and Klebold who committed suicide after perpetrating the worst massacre in a high school in the history of the United States.

How could I write about Buffy's metaphorical battles in the face of statements like that of Columbine survivor Brooks Brown: "I'm just insanely confused… I mean, I'm suffering four losses of close friends. And two of those killed the other two. And I just can't figure out why" (quoted in Olson 123)?

And yet, bizarrely it seemed to me at the time, a connection developed between the massacre and the TV show. The publication date of one of the *Buffy* series of books was put off for several months; the stand-alone episode entitled "Earshot" was cancelled; and "Graduation Day, Part II" of the season finale was postponed in the United States.

The book postponement did not generate much public response. The April 27, 1999, cancellation of "Earshot" evoked some grumbling from *Buffy* fans, but since (a) the episode was originally scheduled to be viewed just seven days after the massacre, (b) it dealt overtly with a potential school shooting, and (c) an episode of *Promised Land* was cancelled for the same reason, fans appeared to sympathize and did not respond with any concrete action. However, over a month after the massacre, The WB revealed at the last minute their decision to postpone the viewing of the second half of "Graduation Day" (scheduled for May 25) until after the high school graduation season. This engendered a huge response, especially since the first half had been screened on May 18, and it had a cliffhanger ending. Further fuelling the sense of outrage among fans was the fact that "Graduation Day, Part II" had aired in Canada on May 24, the day before it was cancelled in the United States.

In frustration, and indulging what he himself termed a "Grateful Dead moment," producer Joss Whedon told fans to record the show illegally: "bootleg the puppy," he urged (Byrne). Stars issued press releases chiding Warner Brothers for blaming TV programming ("Don't Blame TV;" Ostow). Fans started a "Stand Up for *Buffy*" campaign and raised funds for a full-page notice in the June 18th Hollywood edition of *Entertainment Weekly* which pointed out that there was no direct cause-and-effect relationship between *Buffy the Vampire Slayer* and the shooting; Harris and Klebold were not watchers of the show. Their tastes tended toward more nihilistic imaginative worlds like the computer game Doom (Taylor "Digital Dungeons" 42) and the 1994 movie *Natural Born Killers* (Chisholm 23). *Buffy* chat rooms and websites exploded with indignation; one fan wrote "We are the people. We have the Internet. We have the power. Any questions?" (Byrne).

Suddenly my focus was co-opted from a purely literary analysis of the Gothic nature of *Buffy the Vampire Slayer* – an analysis undertaken by several scholars, though not exactly as I'd envisioned it (see Bloustien, Early, Lippert, and Pender) – to a quest to understand the connection between the very real horrors of a high school shooting and the fictional depiction of an underdog hero triumphing over evil and failing math. On the face of it, the relationship is simple: because of the massacre, studio executives overreacted and "Graduation Day, Part II" was postponed. But, because of the cancellation, fans, producers and actors overreacted in defence of the show. I call these both overreactions because the controversy over *Buffy* programming has all the scope of a "teapot tempest" when considered beside the tragedy at Columbine. I felt I could not simply bring a typical academic "compare and contrast" lens to my new project; doing so would belittle the events at Columbine by contextualizing them alongside an hour-long comedy/horror television show. It was with some trepidation, then, that I embarked on a catholic web of research, a web that included predictable elements – vampires as myths and metaphors, Gothic attributes in literature and in high school culture – as well as unexpected ones – the physiology and psychology of blood, chaos theory – all of which were necessary for making some kind of sense of the otherwise inexplicably vehement reactions to the decision to postpone "Graduation Day, Part II."

Literature Review Circa 1999: A Chaotic Welter

When I began my research, I found a lot of information on *Buffy the Vampire Slayer*, but most of it was studio-generated hyperbole; until I found the anthologies *Buffy the Vampire Slayer and Philosophy: Fear and Trembling in Sunnydale* and *Athena's Daughters: Television's New Women Warriors*, *Buffy* was not an easy subject for my academic research. One of the earliest scholarly sources available was Michael Ventura's 1998 *Psychology Today* article "Warrior Women," which draws direct connections between the horror fantasy of fictional Sunnydale High and the difficulties which inhere in non-fictional high school culture in North America:

> The symbolism is dizzying. Drugs, alcohol and gangs are conspicuously absent from Buffy's high school, but it's clear that these are Hell Mouth's vomitus. Demons are the gangs. The surreal transformations in gullible kids victimized by demons – that's your brain on drugs. And the helplessness of grown-ups in the face of this Hell – that's life. (59–60)

Ventura groups *Buffy* with other shows featuring strong heroines like the eponymous *Xena: Warrior Princess* and *La Femme Nikita*, ultimately suggesting that:

America isn't ready to accept sexual ambivalence in its male action heroes. America still wants them to make clear moral choices, even if they have to struggle to get there. None of this half-angel, half-devil stuff. In a man, that's still seen as somewhat sinister; in a woman, it's seductive. (63)

Ventura observed that "Humphrey Bogart, trapped in Buffy's high school, would get drunk and stay drunk" (62), in part because of the ambiguous morality with which Buffy and her cohort must contend. For example, Buffy works hard to use her powers for good, even after she discovers they partake in the very demon magic she fights. At the beginning of season five, she encounters Dracula, and, as Rob Cover observes in "From Butler to Buffy: Notes Towards a Strategy for Identity Analysis in Contemporary Television Narrative":

She is told by Dracula – our cultural authority on all things vampiric and demonic – that her powers are "rooted in darkness" and that he has indeed searched the world for "a creature whose darkness rivals my own" ("Buffy vs. Dracula," 5x01). In the episode "Get it Done," (7x15), the [slayer] powers are indeed revealed to be demonic in origin, the essence of a demon given to the slayers by ancient sorcery.

Thus, Ventura's early observation that Buffy's power is rooted in ambiguity is borne out in subsequent seasons.

In magazines, Buffy tended to be applauded as a positive role model for young girls, though not without reservations. *HUES*'s Anamika Samanta and Erin Franzman cite the discontinuity most strongly:

There's nothing wrong with using a pretty actress, and Gellar is great as Buffy. It's even fair to say that kickboxing in platform heels is pretty fierce.... But the show takes one step forward and one step back by objectifying its star in this manner. No one notices that Buffy is the smartest, strongest (literally and figuratively) teen role model television has seen in ages. Instead, the show gets attention for its Lolita-esque star's abundant cleavage. (Samanta and Franzman 28–31)

Or, as Barbara Lippert asks in *New York*: "So is Buffy an epochal figure for independent women? Or is she simply Donna Reed with cleavage and a gift for impaling?" (25). The contrast between Buffy's performance of frailty and actual strength in mind and body continues to intrigue scholars; while some like Patricia Pender situate Buffy as a feminist icon for whom "kicking ass is comfort food" (164; see also Marinucci), others focus on her need to perform weakness and obedience (Early 64; Tjardes 76) – a need which she largely overcomes in season five, when she becomes the main caregiver of her sister, Dawn (O'Reilly 276–78). Though most of these articles either laud or denigrate Buffy as a role model for the high school demographic, none is particularly helpful in grappling with the ways that Sunnydale High's location on the Hellmouth may help with a discussion of the Columbine massacre.

Commentaries by a variety of news reporters, magazine columnists and actors from the show were slightly more useful in coming to an understanding of why episodes of *Buffy* were cancelled in Columbine's wake, though the sheer quantity of coverage was overwhelming. These reports had one thing in common: each and every one grappled unsuccessfully with the question of why such an event could happen, trying out various possible explanations and finding them lacking. On the Canadian front, Andrew Phillips observed in his *Maclean's* article "Lessons of Littleton":

Champions of family values bemoaned the decline of same. Media critics criticized the media for polluting the culture with images of violence. And, of course, proponents and opponents of gun control conducted their own well-rehearsed verbal shootout. (18–19)

Actors got into the discussion; pointing the finger at the United States' National Rifle Association was *Buffy* regular Seth Green who stated, "Well, if you want a target, let's look at the gun lobbies that have so much power in Washington that they keep the Congress, the president and the people from really addressing the situation" (quoted in "Don't blame TV, Says Buffy Vampire"). Reporter Richard Corliss wrote in *TIME* magazine, "Flash: movies don't kill people. Guns kill people" (42). In direct contrast to Green's and Corliss's statements, the firearms lobby "was leaning hard…on the theory that guns don't kill people, kids raised on blood-drenched movies, shoot-em up video games and death-obsessed Internet sites do" (Geddes 23). While not defending gun lobbies, an article in *The Economist* included a quote from a Columbine survivor, who felt the blame should be shared with the promulgators of violence in the poplar media: "As one junior student said, with a reference to a Keanu Reeves film: 'One of the guys pulled open his trench coat and started shooting. It was a scene right out of the movie *Matrix.*'" ("The lesson nobody learns" 25). This confusion between filmic fantasy and lived life suggests that Harris and Klebold were caught up in what Baudrillard called "hell of simulation" which is "no longer one of torture, but of the subtle, maleficent, elusive twisting of meaning" (18), a twisting which ultimately involved everyone at the school, and in the media circus which followed.

Because Harris and Klebold wore trench coats and painted their fingernails black, early reports identified them as goths: "The high-school killers were part of a small group styled 'the Trench-Coat Mafia'. They wore long black trench coats, whatever the weather; affected a 'Gothic' look with white make-up" ("The lesson nobody learns" 25). People who partook in that subculture grew concerned about potential backlash and denied that Harris and Klebold were true goths:

The initial assumption that Eric Harris and Dylan Klebold were Goths…got real Goths everywhere hot under the black leather collar. "Teenagers tend to go after the most powerful images they can," explains Seth Baker, a Los Angeles Goth. "They put together a lot of images." Real Goths have nothing to do with violence.

Still, if Klebold and Harris were wolves in Goth's clothing, there was plenty to identify with. "We romanticize the darkness of Humanity," says Peter Stover, 21, a photography major at Chicago's Columbia College, who has midnight blue hair and regulation pale skin. "We're creatures of the night." (Taylor "We're Goths and Not Monsters" 37)

Then there are those who felt that the responsibility for school shootings in general, and Columbine in particular, ultimately rested not in the culture but on the shoulders of people responsible for censoring that culture in the home, namely, parents. In response to the cancellation of "Graduation Day, Part II," Sarah Michelle Gellar – the actor who plays Buffy – stated, "Those who seek to blame television should 'look closer to home.' TV's job is to entertain, she said, not to teach children their lessons" (quoted in Ostrow). Linked to the conservative trend towards strong family values was the idea that ties within communities needed to be strengthened, especially where criminals were concerned. For example, Harley Phillips, the former police chief and mayor of Taber, Alberta – site of a copycat killing on April 28, 1999 – said that he was "far more concerned with what he describes as the lax treatment of young criminals by the courts. He also sees a need for families and communities across the country to reflect on their priorities" (Bergman 23). Finally, some effectively despaired of ever understanding events such as Columbine or Taber. Alberta Education Minister Gary Mar said: "No rational act can ever overcome irrational behaviour" (Bergman 23). Thus, attempts to assign blame for the Columbine tragedy ran the gamut from finger pointing at the media, movies and television, the NRA, goth culture, home culture, communities and criminal courts to amorphous generalizations about rationality.

According to Fred Botting in his book *Gothic*, the very multiplicity of possible reasons for the Columbine shooting indicate that it was an intrinsically Gothic event: "Uncertainties about the nature of power, law, society, family and sexuality dominate Gothic fiction. They are linked to wider threats of disintegration manifested most forcefully in political revolution" (Botting 5).

Hellmouth as Strange Attractor

The term "chaos" arises both in the fictional world of *Buffy the Vampire Slayer* and in reports and editorials about the Columbine massacre. In *Buffy*, chaos is a particular demon dimension; there are chaos demons, and one minor human character, Ethan Rayne, worships chaos. Rayne is an untrustworthy trickster figure who functions as a catalyst for episode-long destabilizing events like causing all the adults in Sunnydale to regress into their high school personae ("Band Candy"), transforming Buffy into a spineless Romance heroine ("Halloween") or turning Giles into a demon ("A New Man"). Chaos is similarly present though not central in the reportage of the Columbine massacre. For example, a cynical squib by Lance Morrow of *TIME* magazine used the term "chaos theory" in reference to the "why" questions surrounding Columbine: "The evil effect is evident – innocent blood everywhere; the cause, in the case of Littleton anyway, remains obscure. Evil is, after all, a mystery. The uniqueness of individual evils owes something to chaos theory" (43).

Although the use of the word "chaos" in *Buffy* generally refers to a mean-spirited tricksterism unrelated to chaos theory, and Morrow's evocation of chaos theory reads more like a trendy allusion than means for understanding, chaos theory actually supplies two concepts helpful in analyzing why "Graduation Day, Part II" was cancelled after Columbine: "iteration" which is discussed in a later section of the essay, and the "strange attractor."

In her book *Chaos Bound: Orderly Disorder in Contemporary Literature and Science*, N. Katherine Hayles explains that strange attractors are "deeply encoded structures" in what otherwise appear to be chaotic situations (9). Specifically, theorists posit the presence of a strange attractor to explain unpredictable phenomena which occur within a bounded, definable situation. In his book *Introduction to Chaos and Coherence*, physicist Jan Frøyland states: "Even if the motion is chaotic the orbit may nevertheless be bounded in all directions in phase space and attracted to geometrical objects called *strange attractors* with strange and unfamiliar properties" (3). Though the concept of the strange attractor was developed to describe movement among molecules, the idea has been appropriated by literary and cultural theorists to describe situations in which multiple elements operate in an apparently unpredictable manner, but with partially predictable results. Where a strange attractor operates, unexpected things happen within known parameters.

There were seven shootings in middle-class high schools in the United States and Canada between 1997 and 1999: in Pearl, Mississippi; West Paducah, Kentucky; Jonesboro, Arkansas; Edinboro, Pennsylvania; Fayetteville, Tennessee; Springfield, Oregon; and Taber, Alberta ("The lesson nobody learns" 25). Despite the number of shootings, there is no way to predict when or where high school shootings will occur; that they will occur is evident. This sounds like a "strange attractor" operates within American high school culture.

Buffy creator Joss Whedon recognized that there is a predictable element to the chaotic incidents of violence that take place in high schools, though he doesn't call it a "strange attractor." He calls it the Hellmouth:

The Hellmouth came from my friend Tommy and me sitting around saying, you know, we need a reason why every monster in history would come to Sunnydale. The Hellmouth became sort of the central concept for us because it allows us to get away with anything.

Sunnydale High is based on every high school in America because so many kids feel like their school is built on a Hellmouth. What makes the show popular is the central myth of high school as horrific. The humiliation, the alienation, the confusion of high school is taken to such great proportions that [they] become demonic. (Whedon "Welcome to the Hellmouth" interview)

For example, a recurring character named Jonathan is first featured centrally in season three's episode "Earshot" (the first episode cancelled in the wake of Columbine) when he brings a gun to school, planning on killing himself because he has been bullied and made the butt of jokes for many years. (e.g., in season three's "The Wish," when Cordelia tries to return to popularity after dating Xander, the "in" clique she's trying to rejoin taunts her with the possibility of moving on to Jonathan). That bit of taunting is similar to the bullying experienced by Eric Harris and Dylan Klebold. Their friend Brooks Brown remembers seeing them dodge rocks and bottles, brush off taunts, get pushed against lockers (Olson 123). Later, in season four's "Superstar," Jonathan does a spell that endows him with Buffy's strength, and becomes a suave and powerful James Bond–like character, which further aligns him with Eric Harris, who, along with being bullied, had an extreme superiority complex (Cullen). Thus, I posit that there's a strange attractor in any given high school culture and the Hellmouth of *Buffy the Vampire Slayer* is a metaphorical reification of that high school strange attractor. The feelings of alienation and humiliation which the high school strange attractor generates within any school's student body cannot be predicted directly, but the results of its presence – self-directed violence from anorexia to suicide, and/or violent lashing out against others, from bullying to school shootings – are statistically, though not individually, predictable.

Chaos theorists posit the existence of a strange attractor by its effects and then look around for ways to understand how it functions so that it will become less strange. Michael R. Bütz's article "The Vampire as a Metaphor for Working with Childhood Abuse" provides some insights which transfer from the subject of his study – childhood abuse – to the subject of my study – abuse among young adults at high school. Bütz notes:

> Questions remain about why our culture is so fascinated with the vampire, what it is about this mythic creature that so resonates with the psyche of our culture. A possible reason for its hold on our collective imagination lies in the vampire's resemblance to the physically or sexually abusive individuals in our society. The metaphor of the vampire may illuminate the tragic interchange between abuser and abused so as to lead to a deeper psychological understanding of abusive situations. (426)

Bütz speaks of abuse trauma as linked to a private event or series of events, and of the originating abuser as a maladjusted individual embedded in the victim's imagination as a vampire. In contrast, in Whedon's fictive world, the trauma is specific to a public location (high school), and the abusers are usually not individuals but groups – from in cliques at school to their demonic equivalents in *Buffy*. Thus, "The Vampire as a Metaphor for Working with Childhood Abuse" provides one reason for the inexplicably vehement responses to the cancellation of "Graduation Day, Part II" in the wake of Columbine. The show's assumption that high school has the attributes of hell, similar to those of childhood abuse trauma – to those embroiled, it is horrible, apparently inescapable, seemingly eternal – is too correct, too reflective of lived life, for it to be unaffected by the real high school shooting.

The hellishness of high school partakes in a social stratification so persistent that it achieves a mythic inevitability. Brooks Brown pointed out that "the jocks in our school, they're treated like gods, and they treat everyone else like crap" (quoted in Olson 123). After the shootings, Columbine students finished their year at another local school, Chatfield. One student wrote:

> If you had been to any of our sporting events against Chatfield, you'd know that there is a huge rivalry between our schools. Welcoming us the way they did was an incredibly generous gesture.
>
> …To begin the day, we had a huge assembly with all the Columbine faculty and students. We sang our school song and screamed, "WE ARE! COLUMBINE!" as a way to restore our sense of school pride, courage and strength. (Bane 126)

Inviting Columbine students to share their school was common decency on the part of Chatfield: that this student thought it was "an incredibly generous gesture" suggests that the culture of competition and stratification remained in place even after the shooting. Furthermore, the assembly reinforcing Columbine students' identification with their school entrenched the very differentiation that led another student to say of the pre-massacre atmosphere at Columbine: "You have to understand that there were as many lies, rumours and intrigues [at the high school] as in Washington this past year.… It's almost the definition of a teenager to be cruel to those who are not like you" (quoted in Gibbs 27). Nor is there any evidence of substantive positive change since the school reopened on August 16, 1999:

Inside the school, bullet and shrapnel holes have been plastered and painted over. New lockers block the entrance to the library where 10 people died.

"That's the creepiest part of all," said student Kim Blair. "The library is just gone."

In an effort to give the school a new feel, construction crews renovated its interior, painting the formerly grey walls white, green and blue and replacing carpet in the school's sprawling corridors with white tile.

"I think [the changes] will make it easier for kids who saw things," said Lindsey Neam, a senior. "But for others, it might just make it harder, because kids just want things to be the same. They want to get back to normal." (McDowell A15)

Nowhere in this comment is there any acknowledgment that the "normal" state of affairs at Columbine – where bullying was tolerated and cruelty was considered *de rigueur* – may have been a contributing factor leading to the shooting. The implication is that high school was, is, and ever shall be, a mouth of hell.

Buffy the Vampire Slayer retrenched that perception weekly. Although individual characters may mature, any social change is inevitably for the worse. The most obvious example came in a season three episode called "The Wish," when a demon grants Cordelia's wish that Buffy Summers had never come to Sunnydale. The result is a depopulated school and a terrified town run by vampires about to open up an abattoir for harvesting the blood of the few humans still alive. In the imaginative world of *Buffy* the best hope is to maintain the status quo, a trait which William Patrick Day notes as an earmark attribute of the Gothic imagination:

The tradition does not offer a vision of imaginative transcendence, nor does it suggest that imagination is capable of the power of transcendence. The Gothic imagination returns us to where we started with no final resolution, for resolutions lie, not in the imagination, but in the world in which the imagination functions. (192)

Joss Whedon's idea of the Hellmouth opening in Sunnydale High mirrors a bit too accurately the lived experience of many middle-American high school students. Buffy's fictive school bears an eerily close resemblance to Columbine, down to the specific site of the library – the opening to *Buffy's* fictitious Hellmouth, and the place in Columbine High School where ten people died.

Symbolic Monsters, Real Blood

Demons, most of which are vampires, persistently infiltrate Sunnydale High. One implication of psychiatrist R. Gottlieb's discussion of vampire mythology, in reference to one of his patients, is that the same could be said of Columbine, metaphorically. His patient's self-description as a vampire applies equally to Eric Harris and Dylan Klebold:

> The story's vampire experienced herself as excommunicated, an outcast, hopelessly damned, miserable, agitated, and dangerous to those very loved ones who had cast her out. It was a story of the wreaking of death, pestilence, and dismemberment upon those loved ones… Above all, it was a story of *revenance* – of a return from the dead, from the grave – of a loved person who had been unscathed by the experience of burial and decay. In this way it also became a story of immortality, a story in which permanent loss was not possible. (469)

Thus, the psychological vampire's violent action is actually a reaction to repudiation by those who have spurned as worthless someone they should have recognized as worthy. Of course, the feeling that no one understands you is a signature aspect of adolescent angst, which can only be exacerbated by participation in "the venomous culture that these boys [Harris and Klebold] soaked in – but many kids drink those waters without turning into mass murderers" (Gibbs 33). In terms of immortality – whether or not the Columbine perpetrators understood the finality of death, immured as they were in the fantasy resurrections of video games – in the end they achieved not the eternal life of the vampire but monstrous infamy.

In another form of the vampire's metaphorical place in contemporary culture, Cyndy Hendershot observes that the vampire body "bears an almost identical resemblance to the 'normal' human body" (23). The fiction that monsters walk among us – indistinguishable from humans until they choose to reveal themselves, usually at the point of maximum destruction – provides a powerful explanation for the actions of perpetrators like Harris and Klebold, and an answer to the question "how could a school not know the hatred in its halls was more than routine teenage alienation?" (Gibbs 34). By this logic, school authorities couldn't have known, because the perpetrators were monsters in human guise. Unfortunately, it is a logic that applies only in fiction.

The depiction of the bloody aftermath of the Columbine shooting – which led one Buffy fan to observe "People seem to think that it's fictional television that's [sic] bad. What about all the news coverage of the shooting and the students talking about what happened? That's muc [sic] more graphic" (marissa joy, email message to author) – unintentionally brought the massacre into closer congruency with vampirism and with *Buffy*. The old newspaper truism "if it bleeds it leads" can be updated to "if it bleeds it feeds" the media need for graphic news coverage twenty-four hours a day.

The notion of blood as food became integral to the myth of the vampire only with the 1897 publication of Bram Stoker's *Dracula*; in his article "The Stressful Kiss: A Biopsychosocial Evaluation of the Origins, Evolution and Societal Significance of Vampirism," Donald R. Morse states that, since *Dracula*, an "important aspect of the vampire belief is blood, the essence of life, vitality, and strength. Vampire means blood monster" (183). Gottlieb also states that a primary aspect of the vampire tale as we tell it today is "intense needfulness, characterized at times as parasitic or destructive, cast primarily as a need for nutriment or sustenance" (51); certainly the most uncanny food imaginable is the lifeblood of a human. The Buffy mythology exploits this tradition: for example, in "The Dark Age," Buffy calls a hospital blood delivery truck "Vampire meals-on-wheels" (Golden and Holder 16). Consequently when *TIME* magazine's Lance Morrow pinpoints the effect of evil as "innocent blood everywhere" (43), he reinforces the vampire characterization of Harris and Klebold who penetrated the bodies of their victims with bullets, not fangs.

Prior to Bram Stoker's *Dracula*, "European vampires...sometimes sucked blood, but not always. Some did not suck blood at all" (Gottlieb 469). Instead, vampire was one of the names given to a revenant that returned to haunt familiar abodes and, in so doing, destroyed loved ones by sapping their energy – a rationalization for a decline in health due to grief (470). These pre-Stoker vampires leeched vigour from their victims, leaving them enervated and exhibiting the symptoms of a wasting disease, which explains why "part of the vampire belief was related to the spread of infections such as the plague. In the Middle Ages, it was considered that vampirism was similar to a contagious disease" (Morse 183, see also Gottlieb 469–70). The blood of a person bitten by a vampire therefore becomes an infectious venom. Among the reports on Columbine was that of Nancy Gibbs, also writing in *TIME* magazine, who wondered "what turned two boys' souls into poison?" (25–26), merging the symbolic notion of soul with the reality of blood. Morse's article goes on to list diseases which have traditionally been related to vampirism – *Hematodipsia*, pernicious anemia, congenital porphyria, congenital syphilis, and "finally there are psychopaths who have no allegiance to vampirism, except that vampires could be considered as serial killers" (192). In Morse's paradigm, "vampires" like Harris and Klebold are vectors of psychopathy infecting an unsuspecting populace.

Prior to the Columbine massacre, school officials failed to act on the monstrous potential of Harris and Klebold because, like uncanny vampires, they appeared to be human. There's a simple reason for that, though; the boys were human, not vampires in either the "disease-vector" or "blood-drinking, immortal monster" sense. Unlike vampires, and despite their lasting infamy, Harris and Klebold died when they fired into their own heads. The only appetite sustained by all the blood they spilled was that of the twenty-four hour news cycle.

Michel Foucault's observation in volume one of *The History of Sexuality* that, historically, "blood was *a reality with a symbolic function*" (147) is unexpectedly borne out both within Columbine, and in Columbine's relation to *Buffy*. That Foucault is speaking of the familial bloodlines does not change the aptness of his statement in the current context; the Columbine victims' blood was both tragically real and demonstrative of the power that two erstwhile geeks wielded over their more socially successful peers. Blood is also the major element in common between the lives lost on the floor of the Columbine library, and the symbolic hell under the floor of the library at Sunnydale High, which is accessed by soaking it in someone's lifeblood ("Conversations with Dead People").

Foucault goes on to state that sexuality has largely replaced blood as a mechanism of power in contemporary culture: "The new procedures of power that were devised during the classical age and employed in the nineteenth century were what caused our societies to go from *a symbolics of blood to an analytics of sexuality*" (148). Included in the "analytics of sexuality" is the theme of health and normalcy in both the individual and social bodies, as contrasted to concerns with "law, death, transgression, the symbolic, and sovereignty" (148), which characterize a culture based on bloodlines. But as Botting points out in regard to Francis Ford Coppola's 1992 movie *Bram Stoker's Dracula*, issues of sexuality, inextricable from those of health, are vexed in contemporary culture:

> Sexuality, linked to violence and death, again threatens humanity with the sublime and vampiric spectre of its imminent dissolution: both global and microscopic, the threat is simultaneously internal and external, crossing all borders with impunity and uncanny effects. Invading from without and destroying from within, the AIDS virus breaks the cellular defences of individual organisms and leaves its sufferers in an emaciated limbo.
>
> The patterns of repetition and the condition that repetition implies are belied by the film's artificial claims to authenticity. (177)

The mythology of *Buffy* is haunted by the spectre of the AIDS virus just as the plagues prompted the genesis of vampire myths: Buffy's sweetheart Angel is a vampire with a soul. If he experiences one moment of true happiness – such as when he has sex with Buffy in season two – he'll lose that soul and become a monster again. Thus the show preaches abstinence to its teenaged audience, and the character of Buffy acts as a conceptual nexus point – for the symbolics of blood, law, transgression and death involved with vampire myths; for the sexual objectification of desire and its attendant anxieties over health and death; and given her appearance in millions of households every week, for technological iteration.

Gothic Iterations

The second concept I borrow from chaos theory is iteration. N. Katherine Hayles describes iteration's importance to chaos theory as follows:

> The fundamental assumption of chaos theory...is that the individual unit does not matter. What does matter are recursive symmetries between different levels of the system.... It is a systemic approach, emphasizing overall symmetries and the complex interactions between microscale and macroscale levels. (169–70)

The difference between simple repetition and the more adaptable iteration rests in the concept of scale; iterations are repetitions in varying gradations. Also inherent in iteration is the idea of self-similarity or, as James Gleick defines it in his textbook *Chaos: Making a New Science*, "symmetry across scale [which] implies recursion, pattern inside of pattern" (103).

The Columbine shooting had the highest body and injury count among the seven high school shootings between 1997 and 1999. Less self-similar iterations – but still crucial because our knowledge of them is almost always mediated, literally – are news stories generated by Columbine and the other violent incidents. Then there are the fictions, marketed as such, based on these and similar stories, including *Buffy*. There are also the two pre-iterations most intimately involved with the Columbine massacre: Harris's website, which prior to the shooting was examined for anti-Semitic content by the Simon Wiesenthal Center but not tagged as worthy of action; and a video that Harris and Klebold shot "in which they talked about blowing up the school. It showed them parading through the hallways of Columbine High in their black trench coats, threatening to destroy it, and was shown in one of their classes last fall. But no one saw it as a serious threat" (Phillips 20).

Seen from this point of view, the massacre was not the isolated event that psychologists would have us believe, despite this quote published in *Teen People* shortly after Columbine: "'Schools are enormously safe,' says Laurence Steinberg, Ph.D., a professor of psychology at Temple University.... 'These events get a lot of attention only because they *are* rare'" ("Getting Past the Fear" 125–27). Rather, school shootings are one aspect of a violent narrative mimetically repeated across the scales of North American culture, from the personal, through high school, all the way to the pan-accessible globalized culture of public media and cinematic fiction.

Given these repetitions, school shootings invite Gothic description, since, as Eugenia C. DeLamotte observes in *Perils of the Night: A Feminist Study of Nineteenth-Century Gothic*, "repetition is so central an aspect of the [Gothic] genre that it may be considered one of its major conventions" (24). Gothic texts manifest the scaling characteristic of iteration in that they describe social manifestations of private "demons":

> The Gothic vision has from the beginning been focused
> steadily on social relations and social institutions… Its
> simultaneous focus on the most private demons of the psyche
> can never be separated from this persistent preoccupation
> with the social realities from which those demons always, in
> some measure, take their shape. (DeLamotte vii)

DeLamotte expands upon iteration as "deadly" in her discussion of Nathaniel Hawthorne's writing, an uncanny description of the world Harris and Klebold may have inhabited:

> Hawthorne's sinners are afraid of revealing their secrets
> and therefore fear the intrusion of others into their private
> world. Thus they are cut off from other people, from nature
> in its true aspect, and from God. But their nightmarish
> separateness is, paradoxically, also a nightmarish unity.
> The whole world is a terrible oneness for them because
> it is a deadly iteration of their own perceiving minds, a
> multitudinous echo of the self. (98–99)

In the *Buffy* mythology, when you are turned by a vampire, "you die. And a demon sets up shop in your old house. And it walks and talks and remembers your life, but it's not you" (quoted in Holder 196, from the episode "Lie to Me"). Gloria Bloustien calls the Buffyverse vampires' infestation of human hosts mimetic, which she defines as a "transformation by which a copy of something draws power from the original in order to assume its power.... Television is a particularly important vehicle for this process (Bloustien 432). *Buffy*'s vampires – as scaled down, psychological iterations of the social high school Hellmouth – are chaotic, and Gothic, and eerily convincing patterns upon which the monstrousness of people like Harris and Klebold can be conceptually moulded.

According to chaos theorist Ira Livingston in his book *Arrow of Chaos: Romanticism and Postmodernity*, it is information – not disenfranchised high school students – which has gone viral, and technology – not blood – which is the root of power. Speaking of the internet, he says: Postmodern power-knowledge has been "rendered *viral*.... The virus is an episteme with a vengeance: globally dispersed but at a microscopic scale, it is 'big-little'" (5). Information, like "how to make pipe bombs," is replicated and dispersed on the internet, where Harris accessed it, and the source of power for contemporary vampires is not Foucauldian blood but Livingstonian information flowing through the internet where the uncontrolled iteration of information is tantamount to viral infection.

All these repetitions – multiple schools that experienced shootings; the iterations of these shootings in the news and in narrative; the fictional infestation of humans by monsters as metaphors for the shooters' inhumanity; the global iteration of the most minute pieces of knowledge, itself an iteration of the lifeblood which feeds vampires – open up to Gothic interpretation both the Gothic horror-comedy of *Buffy the Vampire Slayer*, and the plain horror of the Columbine massacre.

Hero-Monster Iterations

Monstrousness is not limited to the bad guys in *Buffy the Vampire Slayer*; Buffy herself shares traits with the vampires she hunts. In "'Buffy vs. Dracula"'s Use of Count Famous," Tara Elliott observes "Buffy is as strong, physically and mentally, as Dracula, but not stronger." Season six explores the demonic source of Buffy's power through her sado-masochistic relationship with the vampire Spike: "the microchip implanted in his brain that causes him pain when he hurts other humans will not respond when he treats her violently. Buffy seems transformed into a monster, like Spike and his fellow vampires, with whom he is able to follow his impulses without restraint" (Siegel 59). Clearly Buffy is not just a latter-day sheriff ridding Sunnydale of its criminal monsters; being the slayer has monstrous implications in and of itself.

For one thing, her fated role as the slayer isolates her from her peers; Craigo-Snell pointed out that as early as "3.18, *Earshot*, Willow says of Buffy, 'She's hardly even human anymore'" (note 15). Whedon states, "I've always been interested in vampires, I think because of the isolation they feel. They're in the world but not of it…. Buffy deals with that kind of alienation" ("Angel" interview). This helps explain why the vampires she slays explode into dust; he says "it shows that they're monsters. I didn't really want to have a high school girl killing people every week" (ibid.).

Whedon's other reasons for the explosion of vampire bodies – because it's convenient ("you don't have to clean up bodies for twenty minutes at the end of every show") and because it "looks really cool" (ibid.) – indicate that Buffy's ferocity is not of primary importance to him, although she does tend to problem solve through violence. In "Killed by Death," when her friend Xander protests, "You don't know how to kill this thing," Buffy suggests, "I thought I might try violence," to which he replies, "Solid call" (quoted in Golden and Holder 12). Similarly, in "Inca Mummy Girl," she tells Xander, "I don't always use violence, do I?" and he mock-mollifies her by saying, "The important thing is, you believe that" (quoted in Golden and Holder 22), because she does, and it makes her frighteningly similar to the demons she dusts.

The villain of season four is a self-similar iteration of Buffy, a creature named Adam who is composed of human-designed technology and parts cannibalized from various demons; as such he is a contemporary Frankenstein's creature. They are similar in that just as Buffy was under the authority of the Watchers' Council, so too Adam was intended to be a weapon for the Initiative, a covert arm of the United States military. Both Buffy and Adam grew beyond the expectations of their governing organizations, largely due to their demon-rooted powers and unexpected intelligence, and both broke away from those organizations.

Both relate to their mentors as child to parent. Professor Walsh forms Adam the way Pygmalion formed his statue, and with much the same obsessiveness; unlike the statue, Adam's first action on being animated is to kill Professor Walsh, while calling her "Mommy" ("The I in Team"), rather than to become her spouse. Buffy, too, is formed by her training with the Watchers' Council through Giles who fulfills a paternal role in regard to his charge. When slayer and watcher realize that the council's traditional methods of training are not only ineffective but actually endanger Buffy ("Helpless"), Giles breaks with the council and remains loyal to Buffy, continuing to train and form her abilities without their support. Thus Giles is akin to Pygmalion in that he takes a formless "bimbo" (Whedon quoted in Lippert 25) and shapes someone marvellous from that blank beginning. However, Buffy is unlike Pygmalion's statue in every way but personal beauty; she is independent, resourceful, strives to be honourable, constantly able to improvise weapons from what comes to hand, verbally forthright and the thought of Giles as anyone's lover gives her the willies. Unlike Pygmalion's statue, she has a name; not only that, but the show is named after her rather than being called *Giles and the Vampire Slayer*, which would be the equivalent to Ovid's "Pygmalion and the Statue."

The demonic source of Buffy's powers, her identification with demonic characters – an identification which increases over the seasons – and her tendency to solve crises through violence align Buffy not only with the vampires she stakes but also with the perpetrators of the Columbine shooting. If heroic Buffy is in essence a monster, then it is possible that Eric Harris and Dylan Klebold were heroes gone horribly wrong, film noir Robin Hoods standing up for the rights of the disenfranchised in what should have been a nigh-inconceivable way, were it not for the commingling of fantasy and reality that Baudrillard decries (12–14).

Ambivalence towards Buffy's violent tendencies plays out in the statement attributed to Sarah Michelle Gellar after the cancellation of "Graduation Day, Part II":

> I share the WB network's concern and compassion for the recent tragic events at Columbine High School and at academic campuses across the country. I am, however, disappointed that the year-long culmination of our efforts will not be seen by our audience.
>
> *Buffy the Vampire Slayer* has always been extremely responsible in its depiction of action sequences, fantasy and mythological situations. Our diverse and positive role models 'battle the horror of adolescence' through intelligence and integrity, and we endeavor to offer a moral lesson with each new episode.
>
> There is probably no greater societal question we face than how to stop violence among our youth. By cancelling intelligent programming like *Buffy the Vampire Slayer*, corporate entertainment is not addressing the problem.

Gellar's articulate defensiveness is partially explained by the fact that this is not the first time such a situation has arisen in her career. She had a cameo role in *Scream II*, the 1997 movie which allegedly inspired

> a sixteen-year-old Lynwood, California boy [to stab] his mother to death with the help of two of his cousins, 14 and 17. Apparently the boys had planned to wear Grim Reaper masks and carry voice-distortion boxes like those in the films, but they couldn't raise enough money to buy the items.
>
> "They're saying the movie made them do it," says Gellar angrily. "I don't buy that. *Scream* is the excuse they are using to get off. It's horrible, but these people should know better. Murder is wrong – people know that. We don't say, 'Do this.' We are entertaining you. Not everything is a public-service announcement." (Dunn 44)

According to Fred Botting, the persistence of Gothic narrative elements in both fiction and lived life renders Gellar's stance naive: "Producing powerful emotions rather than aesthetic judgments, effects on audiences and readers rather than instructions for them, [these] narrative forms and devices spill over from worlds of fantasy and fiction into real and social spheres" (168). Furthermore, Gellar's statement that "murder is wrong – people know that" implies that those who murder are something other than people, a textbook example of the societal desire to classify perpetrators as monsters, and thereby abrogate their status as humans.

Fearful Iteration

There is one significant way in which all the iterations of the massacre at Columbine High School – including those as removed as fictions like *Buffy* – differ from the event, and that is in the residual fear felt by survivors. One student wrote, "I looked at all the people who had come to grieve for Columbine, and I found myself saying 'They know the sorrow, but they'll never know the fear'" (Bane 126). And yet we'll try to know it through vicarious reiteration, most frivolously in horror fictions, as Isaac Tylim explains in "The Vampire Game": "Horror movies in general, and vampire ones in particular, capitalize on the compulsion to repeat traumatic experiences in order to master them" (282). Similarly, William Patrick Day hits upon a crucial motive for consumers of Gothic narratives like *Buffy*, when he says "Gothic fantasy is the expression of the fears and desires created, but unacknowledged, by conventional culture" (177). The hell which is high school is one such fear: its widespread reiteration in popular narratives like *Buffy* does not constitute acknowledgement of the problem so much as exploitation. Sarah Michelle Gellar's defensive statement of *Scream II* is perfectly applicable here: "not everything is a public-service announcement" (Dunn 44). Mass-marketed, pop culture fictions like *Buffy* don't reiterate the hellish high school narrative in order to change it, but to use it; in so doing they entrench it.

Gothic fictions – especially those which mix horror with comedy – are about instilling fear, but a safe fear, like an inoculation: consumers can reassure themselves that "it's fiction." In the case of events like Columbine, the reassurance is less secure, and our refrain is "it can't happen here, Lord, no, it could never happen here" (Gibbs 26). But that is not the case: it can and has happened here. And rather than teaching us how to avoid hell, cultural reiterations like *Buffy the Vampire Slayer* suggest that hell is unavoidable. In such a paradigm, Harris's and Klebold's actions make a terrible kind of sense.

Traditional, Stoker-type vampires replicate themselves through infecting their prey and turning them into predators. But there are two important ways in which they do not iterate; as Hendershot observes: "The vampire's body...cannot cast a shadow or a reflection: it cannot be seen by the person who possesses it" (23). Thus, the difference between Joss Whedon and the perpetrators of Columbine is the difference between reflection and iteration. Whedon says that through *Buffy the Vampire Slayer* he has learned to think differently:

I'm able to look at high school and say, "There's the dumb jock who was mean to me. Well, what's his perspective? He's going through something, too."....

...A lot of times, the story doesn't make sense until we figure out who's suffering and why. Including the bad guy. (Whedon quoted in Golden and Holder 241)

Demonstrating his Gothic sensibility, Whedon recognizes that "whatever horror is out there is not as black and terrible as what is already within and between us," though the emotional core of the fiction that he created "is a very safe place. These are people who really care about one another" (241). In contrast, Harris's psychopathy and Klebold's depression isolated them from any community other than each other, which was hardly caring or safe. Within that limited social economy, they persuaded each other it was right and reasonable to use their considerable intelligence to annihilate the bullies and cronies of Columbine, rather than to understand them. After Columbine, Jefferson County District Attorney David Thomas wondered why "American society seems to be turning out children without feeling or remorse" (Phillips 21), or people who, no matter how intelligent, are unable to reflect upon themselves or to perceive themselves as people whose actions cast real shadows in this world.

Information from Chaos

These then are some reasons for the cancellation of "Graduation Day, Part II," and the disproportionate furor that followed – reasons that go deeper than The WB's desire to generate some free public relations exposure and avoid rocking the boat while President Clinton's anti-violence legislation was debated. First, *Buffy the Vampire Slayer* is a fiction that re-entrenches the myth of high school as hell; Columbine both happened because, and proves that, *Buffy*'s central metaphor – that a Hellmouth underlies high school – is only too accurate, and so the show forces one of those Gothic "fears and desires created, but unacknowledged by conventional culture" (Day 177) into the face of that culture, which simply reacted to repress it.

Second, the perpetrators of the massacre have been cast by the media as virtual vampires, both as intelligent human prey who became intelligent monstrous predators, and as disease vectors capable of replicating not only pipe bombs from instructions on the Web, but copycats like the Taber shooter, though not, it seems, capable of reflecting on their own actions. In both monster-vampire and disease-vampire paradigms, Harris and Klebold appeared to be the same as the conscienceless vampires of *Buffy*.

That appearance is, of course, inaccurate. Despite the "hell of simulation" that Baudrillard asserts operates in American culture, and which annuls all difference between reality and illusion, there are no such things as vampires, and the relationship between abuser and abused is a perverse one in which an act of violence is a gesture of respect – the worse the violence, the greater the implied respect, even love (Bütz 428; see also Gottlieb 469, Massé 239). This societal disease of abuse, so aptly mythologized as vampirism, is in fact, a sad twisted way of expressing compassion. As a character in Thomas Mann's *The Magic Mountain* states, "Any symptom of illness [is] a masked form of love" (126).

Finally, the character of Buffy partakes of the alienation and violence both of the villains she fights, like Adam the constructed anti-Pygmalion's statue, and of the "vampired" perpetrators of Columbine, which generates anxiety that the distinction between heroes and monsters is arbitrary. As an active incarnation of a traditionally passive object of our viewing pleasure – the movie "scream queen" – Buffy exposes that long-entrenched narrative device as subjective. Further, the character provides a link between society's historical structure based on the reality and symbolism of blood – a Gothic structure elucidated by Foucault – with the contemporary preoccupation with an objectified sexuality. As a nexus for these anxiety-producing attributes, Buffy the character is an easy target for cultural controversy and repression. As for *Buffy* the show, Joss Whedon shot film not only in the same place that Harris and Klebold shot their classmates – a high school – but also in a similar symbolic and mythological place, a Hellmouth. For that perspicacity, *Buffy the Vampire Slayer* paid a nominal price.

3.

FLEX AND STRETCH:

The Inevitable Feminist Treatise on *Catwoman*

The Hook

From a Life that was Taken a New One will be Born.

– *Catwoman* Movie Trailer

If the goal of Western feminism's first wave
was to gain recognition that women
are citizens and not chattel.

If the second wave surged up to gain
for women the same rights as men –
to work, over our bodies, under the law.

Then the third hove up from desire
for those same rights *as women*: recognition.
Equality doesn't mean homogeneity.

And the first washed out over its backlash
the dark reputational cloud that obscured
Wollstonecraft-Godwin's work a century after her death,
(bereaved Godwin, penurious, published her journals,
that detailed "promiscuity" to a judgmental world,[1]

so when Edgeworth suggested Barbauld join her in
a women's periodical, Barbauld demurred, saying "We should
possibly hesitate at joining…Mrs. Godwin."[2])

The second wave fell to similar backwashing
like 1989's Montréal massacre at the Polytechnique;
fourteen women, most of whom studied engineering,
felled by a man who shouted "I hate feminists."[3]

The third wave brings its own invidious riptide
at least as powerful as that which drowned Patience
and raised up that Venus-on-an-Air-Conditioner
Catwoman.

The Plot Line

Shy, sensitive Patience Phillips (Halle Berry) designs ads for
cosmetics giant Hedare Beauty which is about to roll out
Beau-line, a revolutionary anti-aging product. Her boss Laurel
Hedare (Sharon Stone) murders Patience after she discovers
that Beau-line has the unfortunate side effect of turning its
consumers to stone when they stop using it.
   In a mystical twist, Patience returns from death as a
sleek and stealthy supernatural creature with no regard for
boundaries. She is mentored into her new identity by crazy cat
lady Dr. Ophelia Powers (Frances Conroy) who explains that,
through the ages, Catwomen have been elusive, autonomous
avatars of the Egyptian cat goddess Bastet.
   Detective Tom Lone (Benjamin Bratt) dangles like a
string toy before Catwoman. When he sees pre-puss Patience
teetering on an air-conditioning unit, he thinks she's a jumper
and tries to rescue her but she's just out there to save a stray.
Poor Tom cannot reconcile his love for girl-next-door Patience
with his fascination for the masked, larcenous and bullwhip-
wielding Catwoman. Despite this, together they manage to
bring the makers of Beau-line if not to justice, precisely, then to
the dark ends that they earned.

Sinkers

"Bast represents the duality in all women:
docile, yet aggressive; nurturing, yet ferocious."

— Ophelia Powers in *Catwoman*

Allude to *Xena: Warrior Princess*,
Veronica Mars, praising the strong
struggle for self of each eponym
in each vicious social fiction.

Quote *Athena's Daughters*[4] to prove
critical credentials. Temper praise
with a caveat re: the generic ghetto.

Raise briefly *Dark Angel*, regrettably grounded
by the shallow pitch of her own narrative arc.

Sneer equally briefly at others, say *Elektra*,
or *True Blood*, outside the genre, but down
with the gender bend and stretch, though
fatally pandering to the pickup fantasy,
girls just wanna….

Then rapture over *Buffy*, especially the high school
seasons, wherein she is powerful in pink.
Mention (*ahem*) your own Buff article, really
not terribly relevant here, though perpetually
about-to-be reprinted.[5]

Quote *Buffy the Vampire Slayer and Philosophy*:
"Buffy is sexy because of her strength,
not in spite of it."[6]

Note that success will rest in any heroine
who attains a wholly female sense of self-
entitlement, despite the "cultural,
psychoanalytic, and fictional expectation
that they *should* be masochistic
if they are 'normal' women…"[7]

because "the intertwining of love and pain
is
not
natural."[8]

By-Catch

"You are a Catwoman, Patience…
But you are not the first."

– Ophelia Powers in the *Catwoman* novelization[9]

"A Kiss Could Change Her Into
a Monstrous Fang-and-Claw Killer!"[10]
(1942, *Cat People*)

      "A Tender Tale of Terror!"[11]
      (1944, *Curse of the Cat People*)

            "To Caress Me is to Tempt Death!"[12]
            (1957, *Cat Girl*)

                  "Men Die! Women Sigh! Beneath
                  that Batcape – he's all man!"[13]
                  (1966, *Batman*)

                  "An Erotic Fantasy about the Animal in Us All."[14]
                  (1982, *Cat People* remake)

Small Fry

"The Bat, The Cat, The Penguin."

– Batman Returns[15]

Michelle Pfeiffer's Selina Kyle–style Cat,
brought to a feline self by her premature demise:
      ever so like the Bat, except for gender
      and wealth, and so, not much like him at all –

           "Bruce… I would– I would love to live with you
           in your castle… forever, just like in a fairy tale…"
             (Batman caresses the back of her head;
             she claws him on the cheek)
          "I just couldn't live with myself,
          so don't pretend this is a happy ending."[16]

      She has to choose[17] – fairy-tale future
      or tortured past. Sad, but her own. She faces

another truth: the mansion ain't big enough
for more than one self-flagellant soul.

He gets the home, car,
help, privilege, cave.

      She gets ambiguous morality,
      fierce independence,

          a singer sewing vacuum[18]
          for that painted-on look

             and the teasing tendency to regard
             the men as prey-mates

          in subsequent litters of comics
          and our destination,

"CATch her in IMAX."[19]
(2004, *Catwoman*)

The Main Catch

"I might not be a hero, but I'm certainly not a killer."

– Catwoman in Catwoman

The credits show seven writers
    but at least fourteen
        stuck their fingers in
            this pie, ten years in the making.[20]
            Michelle Pfeiffer
        Ashley Judd,
    Sean Young
turned down the lead.[21]

Finally, Berry
    got tapped
        trapped
            in a contract.

"In a movie that stinks of pure desperation,
Warner Bros try and reinvent the character...
but just end up with something that you'd
expect to see in a litter tray."[22]

    "The special effects are second rate and
    completely obvious, the direction...is pitiful
    and the Catwoman outfit, while slightly sexy,
    is just plain stupid."[23]

        "In pieces it's pretty good; unfortunately
        you have to look at it all at once on the big screen,
        which means that this movie is a car wreck."[24]

*

        For only the third time in Razzies'[25] history,
        a recipient showed up to accept an award,[26]

    Halle Berry, clutching her 2002 Oscar, said

"First of all, I want to thank Warner Brothers.
Thank you for putting me in a piece of shit godawful movie..."[27]

Trophy Fish

Catwoman epitomizes fantasy:
what every woman would want to be,
who every man would like to be with.

— Halle Berry, "The Making of Catwoman"

Sigh. So
Hollywood-true

and real world–wrong:

as if all men desire
a "who" barely
more than a "what"

and all women want
to be some thing.

(And her end is propped up
on a preposition. Humph.)

The Fillets

"I don't care that the FDA never saw the headaches and the
nausea and the fainting spells. Those are symptoms I can live
with.... With what we stand to make from consumers demanding
their fix, I can live with it being addictive. But these side effects
from the long-term studies... I thought I could live with it.
I can't live with turning people into monsters."

> – Slavicky in *Catwoman* (the inventor of Beau-line beauty cream)

The masochistic pact:
feel like shit but look fantastic.

Guinea-pig pretty girls the first
corporate casualties, Slavicky the third.

Second? Patience herself, flushed from the factory,
accidental witness, incidental victim.

The Prize

"I was everything they wanted me to be.
I was never more beautiful. Never more powerful.
And then I turned forty and they threw me away."

> – Laurel Hedare in *Catwoman*

Snap! See this close-shorn, stunning model,
stony fisted, shattering the glass ceiling

too far gone in fury to see
– oh no! – it's really her floor

cantilevered over eighty stories
of air-conditioned pressure

that shoves her out the very frame
she broke in her ecstatic hubris.

But wait! Will she reach for
the feline whip-hand held out?

No. Laurel chooses to die shattered
over living cracked,

Pygmalion's worst nightmare,
Propoetidean[28] she-sculpture,

done in by cosmetic crazy glue
and (tsk) an un-shee-mly desire

to rod-rule the body corporate.

The Guts

"I was a professor for twenty years, until I was
denied tenure.[*sniff*] Male academia."

— Ophelia Powers in *Catwoman*

Conduit, catalyst,
powerless Ophelia Powers

wears her unshorn hair down,
predictably.

Second Wave's comic cut-out,
priestess of resentment
crazy cat lady,[29]

driven by the distracting honour
of bearing wisdom
like Mary hauled typhoid:

a drab passer-on
who never really partakes.

Powers teaches Patience
she died.

And to be reborn she must
destroy what's left of herself.

Ophelia's Exhortatory Sonnet

OPHELIA: *Càtwomen are nòt contàined by the rùles of socìety;*
   you fòllow your òwn desìres. Thìs is bòth
   a blèssing and a cùrse. You will òften bè alòne
   and mìsunderstòod. Bùt yòu will expèrience
   a frèedom òther wòmen will nèver knòw.
   Yòu are a Càtwoman. Every sìght, every smèll,
   every sòund, incrèdibly hèightened. Fìerce
   independènce, tòtal cònfidence, inhùman rèflexes.

PATIENCE: *Sò, Ì'm not Pàtience ànymore?*

OPHELIA: *Of còurse you àre, chìld.*
   You are Pàtience, ànd you are a Càtwoman.
   Accèpt it, chìld. You've spènt a lìfetime càged.
   By accèpting whò you àre – àll of whò you àre –
   you can bè frèe. And frèedom is pòwer.[30]

The Choice

There are really three characters:
Patience Phillips, Catwoman, and a fusion of the two.

– Halle Berry, "The Making of Catwoman"

Why does she have to choose

between Ophelia Powers' out of control straggle
and   Laurel Hedare's sheer shorn strength

  between "the unremarkable life of an unremarkable woman"[31]
  and   someone whose "goals are larcenous,"[32] but who
        "simply cannot resist the urge to do good"[33]

    between "a woman who can't seem to stop
         apologizing for her own existence"[34]
    and   "a sleek and stealthy creature balancing
         on the thin line between good and bad"[35]
    ?

       Because of
       a man, of
       course.

Bait

CATWOMAN: You like bad girls?
TOM LONE: Only if they like me back. No, listen,
Patience. Bad isn't something that does it for me.
CATWOMAN: Okay. Bad, good. Gotta be something in
between, right? Maybe it's a little more complicated.

– Catwoman

Detective Tom Lone jails his lovely lady
for murder. Thank Bastet
she escapes in time to save his life!

Then takes his advice,
alibis herself by sneaking back
into his life, her prison.

Sport Fishing

TOM LONE: Detective work is like dating. It's all about
the pursuit. But when you catch them...

– Catwoman

You cage 'em.
You keep them safe
so they can be good.

*

"The figure who was supposed to lay horror to rest
has himself become the avatar of horror who strips voice,
movement, property, and identity from the heroine."[36]

90

Catch…

"Look at it this way, Lone. You may have lost
your woman, but at least you got your man."

– Detective #2 in Catwoman

When he first spies her
teetering on a ledge
he rescues *her*

from a real danger (physical instability)
but a false threat (mental instability).

When he last sees her
beating the crap out of Laurel Hedare
she rescues *him*

from a real danger
(*"Don't be stupid, Laurel; you don't want to kill a cop."*)[37]

and a real threat
(*"I'm a woman, Lone. I'm used to doing
all kinds of things I don't wanna do."*)[38]

*

"What finally does lay Gothic horror to rest is the refusal of masculinist
authority as the only reality to which one can turn and return."[39]

...And Release

[Catwoman's voice, over the final scene of Lone reading her letter]:

The day I died was the day I started to live. In my old life,
I longed for someone to see what was special in me.
You did, and for that, you'll always be in my heart.
But what I really needed was for me to see it.
And now I do. You're a good man, Tom.
But you live in a world that has
no place for someone like me.
You see, sometimes
I'm good. Oh,
I'm very
good.
But
sometimes I'm bad.
But only as bad as I wanna be.
Freedom is power. To live a life untamed and unafraid
is the gift that I've been given, and so my journey begins.[40]

Finis

Still, Patience had to push off
to pull on that heroic catsuit

"So, I'm not Patience anymore?"
– Patience Phillips

and after all the argy-bargy triumph over
cosmetics and falsity and corporate evil

"I don't know who you are."
– Tom Lone

and Our Hero's struggle for, her final fragile
contingent attainment of, an integrated identity

"I'm the same girl you were with last night."
– Patience/Catwoman

Catwoman has to leave
Tom, her friends, everything

"You're confusing me with somebody else."
– Catwoman

because a movie can't bust a block if it
shows a world with enough flex and stretch

"I'm Patience Phillips."
– Catwoman[41]

to fit a whole
female hero.

Notes

1. Stuart Curran, "Women readers, women writers," in *The Cambridge Companion to British Romanticism*, ed. Stuart Curran (Cambridge: Cambridge University Press, 1993), 177–95.

2. Anne Thackery Ritchie, "Mrs. Barbauld," *The Cornhill Magazine* 44 (1881): 599, accessed July 2010, http://books.google.ca/books?id=CgrSAAAAMA AJ&lpg=PA597&ots=3n8GU5wzEz&dq=mrs.%20barbauld.%20The%20 Cornhill%20Magazine&pg=PA581#v=onepage&q=mrs.%20barbauld.%20 The%20Cornhill%20Magazine&f=false.

3. Quoted in Adam Jones, "Case Study: The Montréal Massacre," Gendercide Watch, accessed July 2010, http://www.gendercide.org/case_montreal.html.

4. Frances Early and Kathleen Kennedy, eds., *Athena's Daughters: Television's New Women Warriors* (Syracuse, NY: Syracuse University Press, 2003).

5. Kathleen McConnell, "Chaos at the Mouth of Hell: Why the Columbine High School Massacre had Repercussions for *Buffy the Vampire Slayer*," *Gothic Studies* 2, no. 1, (2000): 119–35.

6. The full quote reads "Buffy's twofold status as both Slayer and sex symbol challenges the connection between women's vulnerability and women's sexuality. Buffy is sexy because of her strength, not in spite of it." Mimi Marinucci, "Feminism and the Ethics of Violence: Why Buffy Kicks Ass," in *Buffy the Vampire Slayer and Philosophy: Fear and Trembling in Sunnydale*, ed. James B. South (Peru, Illinois: Open Court Publishing, 2003), 74–75.

7. Michelle A. Massé, *In the Name of Love: Women, Masochism and the Gothic* (Ithaca, NY: Cornell University Press, 1992), 2. Italics in the original.

8. Ibid., 3.

9. Elizabeth Hand, *Catwoman*, novelization of the 2004 *Catwoman* movie (New York: Del Rey, 2004).

10. Tagline from *Cat People*, directed by Jacques Tourneur (New York: RKO Radio Pictures, 1942). "Cat People (1942)," Internet Movie Database, accessed July 17, 2005, http://www.imdb.com/title/tt0034587/.

11. Tagline from *The Curse of the Cat People*, directed by Gunther von Fritsch and Robert Wise (New York: RKO Radio Pictures, 1944). "*The Curse of the Cat People* (1944)," Internet Movie Database, accessed July 17, 2005, http://www.imdb.com/title/tt0036733/.

12. Tagline from *Cat Girl*, directed by Alfred Shaughnessy (Los Angeles: American International Pictures, 1957). "*Cat Girl* (1957)," Internet Movie Database, accessed July 17, 2005, http://www.imdb.com/title/tt0050235/.

13. Tagline from *Batman*, directed by Leslie H. Martinson (Los Angeles: Twentieth Century-Fox Film Corporation, 1966). "*Batman* (1966)," Internet Movie Database, accessed July 17, 2005, http://www.imdb.com/title/tt0060153/.

14. Tagline from *Cat People*, directed by Paul Schrader (New York: RKO Pictures, 1982). "*Cat People* (1982)," Internet Movie Database, http://www.imdb.com/title/tt0083722/.

15. Tagline from *Batman Returns*, directed by Tim Burton (Burbank, CA: Warner Bros. Pictures, 2002). "*Batman Returns* (1992)," Internet Movie Database, accessed July 17, 2005, http://www.imdb.com/title/tt0103776/.

16. *Batman Returns*, directed by Tim Burton (Burbank, CA: Warner Bros. Pictures, 2002), DVD.

17. Gothic plots "erase the process of the masochist's formation in order to point insistently at the happy ending ideology promises." Massé, *In the Name of Love*, 3.

18. "During an A&E Biography, Michelle Pfeiffer said that her Catwoman costume was vacuum sealed once she was fitted into it for scenes, so she actually had only a short amount of time to perform before she would have to have it opened or she could become light headed and pass out." "*Batman Returns* (1992)," Internet Movie Database, accessed July 17, 2005, http://www.imdb.com/title/tt0103776/trivia?tab=tr&item=tr0794241.

19. Tagline from *Catwoman*, directed by Pitof (Burbank, CA: Warner Bros. Pictures, 2004). "*Catwoman* (2004)," Internet Movie Database, http://www.imdb.com/title/tt0327554/.

20. Daniel Waters wrote a script that was massaged over a decade by "Laeta Kalogridis, Theresa Rebeck (credited), Kate Kondell, John Rogers (credited), John D. Brancato (credited), Michael Ferris (credited), Jon Cowan, John O'Brien, David Reynolds, Harley Peyton, Valerie Breiman, Rita Hsiao, and Andrew W. Marlowe." "*Catwoman* (2004)," Internet Movie Database, accessed July 17, 2005, http://www.imdb.com/title/tt0327554/trivia?tab=tr&item=tr0786724.

21. Richard Scheib, review of *Catwoman*, directed by Pitof, Warner Bros. Pictures, Moria: Science Fiction, Horror and Fantasy Film Review, accessed May 7, 2009, http://moria.co.nz/fantasy/catwoman-film-2004.htm.

22. Jamie Kelwick, review of *Catwoman*, directed by Pitof, Warner Bros. Pictures, The Usher Speaks, 2004, http://www.kelwick.karoo.net/TheUsher-Speaks2004/TheUsherSpeaks-Catwoman.htm.

23. Ibid.

24. D.B. Burroughs. "Comments on *Catwoman*." International Movie Database. Accessed July 17, 2005, http://us.imdb.com/title/tt0327554/#comment (site discontinued).

25. The Razzies are the sarcastic alternative awards to the Oscars, honouring the worst in film: "razz" being short for "raspberry."

26. "*Catwoman* (2004)," Internet Movie Database, accessed July 17, 2005, http://www.imdb.com/title/tt0327554/trivia.

27. "Halle Berry accepts Razzie Award," YouTube video, 2:42, from the 25th Annual RAZZIE Awards presented at the Ivar Theatre in Hollywood on February 26, 2005, posted by "razziechannel," January 13, 2011, http://www.youtube.com/watch?v=U-7s_yeQuDg&lr=1.

28. Preceding the Pygmalion story in book ten of Ovid's *Metamorphoses* is the story of the Propoetides; inhospitable women who murdered their guests and were punished by Venus, goddess of love, first by being turned into stone-hearted prostitutes, and later by becoming completely made of stone. The thought of them turned Pygmalion off all women and led him to sculpt the perfect wife instead.

29. *Catwoman*, directed by Pitof (Burbank, CA: Warner Bros. Pictures, 2004).

30. Ibid. Diacritical marks added.

31. Ibid.

32. Ray Tate, review of *Catwoman*, directed by Pitof, Warner Bros. Pictures, Silver Bullet Comic Books #87, accessed July 17, 2005.

33. Ibid.

34. Austin4577@aol.com, "*Catwoman* (2004)," Internet Movie Database, accessed July 17, 2005, http://www.imdb.com/title/tt0327554/plotsummary.

35. Ibid.

36. Massé, *In the Name of Love*, 12.

37. *Catwoman*

38. Ibid.

39. Massé, *In the Name of Love*, 12.

40. *Catwoman*

41. Dialogue *Catwoman*.

4.
DARK ANGEL:

A Recombinant Pygmalion for the Twenty-First Century

"Pygmalion and his Statue" + *Frankenstein* = *Dark Angel*

Myths evolve through time; as Anthony John Harding observes in *The Reception of Myth in English Romanticism*, "it is the process of transformation and reinterpretation that repays study, not the 'original myth,' which, inevitably, we can only 'know' as a reconstruction" (2). The television show *Dark Angel*, created and produced by James Cameron and Charles H. Eglee, represents an evolutionary step in myths about the uncanny origins of human life. The show's heroine is an inadvertent hybrid of Pygmalion's beloved statue from Ovid's *Metamorphoses* and Victor Frankenstein's loathed monster from Mary Shelley's *Frankenstein, or the Modern Prometheus.*

Dark Angel takes place in Seattle in 2019, several years after the United States has been reduced to third world status and military dictatorship by the detonation of an electromagnetic pulse in the atmosphere. The dark angel (Jessica Alba) is known as Max Guevara by her friends at the Jam Pony bike courier company where she works by day; she supplements that legal income with a bit of cat burglary by night. What her friends and co-workers don't know is that up until she was nine years old, she was known only as X5-452.

She came from Manticore, a secret government agency in which her cohort of X5s (fifth generation transgenic crossbreeds) were not just trained but created through recombinant genetics. Max is preternaturally beautiful, unnaturally strong, resilient in extreme environments and able to jump like a cat. She and a number of her fellow X5s escaped and scattered; some were recaptured or killed but several remain free at the opening of the first season. Thus, Max is motivated to find the members of her X5 platoon who remain at large while keeping away from Manticore's agents, led by the ruthless Colonel Donald Lydecker (John Savage). Though a decade has passed since her escape, Max struggles to develop and maintain a personal identity in the wake of Manticore's rigid indoctrinization; in this she is influenced by her erstwhile love interest, cyberjournalist and social activist Logan Cale (Michael Weatherly).

Though there are several allusions to narrative developments in the second season, this essay takes most of its examples from the first, which establishes the relationships between the three characters most important to analysis in light of the Pygmalion myth: Max herself, Logan Cale and Colonel Donald Lydecker. There are no allusions to a third season, because the show was cancelled at the end of the second, despite its unfinished narrative.

Harding argues that one reason to explore chronological reiterations of myths is to determine the preoccupations of the cultures which generated them. For example, *Frankenstein* is subtitled *or the Modern Prometheus*, thereby signalling itself as a revision of that myth. In the classic tale, Prometheus suffers for betraying the Olympian gods, by *aiding* the newly created humans. In Mary Shelley's revision, the Promethean Victor Frankenstein *withholds* aid from the race he is poised to create, to disastrous effect. Thus, *Frankenstein* reiterates Prometheus with a nihilistic cast, concurrently refining and reflecting social insecurity about parental responsibility, and about the speculative sciences and technologies developed in the wake of the eighteenth century's industrial revolution.

At the genesis of the twenty-first century, the Pygmalion myth undergoes a transformation similar to that of Prometheus in the early nineteenth century. In Ovid's version, the sculptor Pygmalion's love for his statue of an ideal woman leads to its animation by the goddess of love; it becomes Pygmalion's wife and the mother of the sculptor's male hero-child, thus providing the means for the artist's social redemption, though the statue itself remains unnamed and is known only by her social roles.

In contrast, in Mary Shelley's *Frankenstein* the narration is largely shared between the creator and the creature and so the creature's subjectivity is somewhat explored. Brilliant scientist Victor Frankenstein decides to animate an intelligent, living being to satisfy his desire for personal glory; Victor says of his project, "a new species would bless me as its creator and source.... No father could claim the gratitude of his child so completely as I should deserve theirs" (55). His hubris leads to disaster. Although Victor chooses the most attractive bits of the corpses that provide the anatomy for his creation, the result is hideous:

> His limbs were in proportion, and I had selected his features
> as beautiful. Beautiful! – Great God! His yellow skin scarcely
> covered the work of muscles and arteries beneath; his hair
> was of a lustrous black, and flowing; his teeth of a pearly
> whiteness; but these luxuriances only formed a more horrid
> contrast with his watery eyes, that seemed almost of the same
> colour as the dun white sockets in which they were set, his
> shrivelled complexion, and straight black lips. (58)

An ineluctable aura of the unnatural clings to Frankenstein's creation, which crossed the border between life and death in the wrong direction. Not only Victor Frankenstein, but the few humans who see the creature invariably recoil from him (117, 122, 123, 169, 172).

From being hated, the creature learns to hate; through the course of the novel the creature applies his considerable intelligence to the destruction of his creator's happiness, by inexorably murdering most of Victor's family and friends.

Frankenstein is a Gothic revision of the Pygmalion myth. Both concern a human who creates an uncanny simulacrum of human life; both creations are animated to become actual intelligent beings. Neither is named, indicating that neither creation's subjectivity is a concern of the creator. However, where Pygmalion demonstrates humility, Victor Frankenstein demonstrates hubris, a tragic flaw in his character from which stems all the disasters that follow, precisely because success has far more mundane repercussions than Victor Frankenstein anticipates. Rather than earning him fame in the scientific community and the undying gratitude of a new race of beings, his project dumps him in the commonplace yet demanding position of parent, a position he categorically rejects:

> I created a rational creature, and was bound towards him, to assure, as far as was in my power, his happiness and well-being. This was my duty; but there was another still paramount to that. My duties towards the beings of my own species had greater claims to my attention. (180)

Where Pygmalion's excessive care for the beautiful statue ultimately leads to his social integration, Victor's refusal to nurture his ugly creature leads to social expulsion for both creature and creator. Mary Shelley's *Frankenstein* thus reinscribes the Pygmalion myth in a manner that illustrates concerns about parenting raised by Mary Shelley's mother, Mary Wollstonecraft, in her *A Vindication of the Rights of Women*, which Shelley was rereading as she wrote *Frankenstein* (Shelley *Journals of Mary Shelley* 97).

Furthermore, while Victor espouses the belief that the creature is innately evil and his determination to destroy it is mandated by Heaven (Shelley *Frankenstein* 179–80), the creature himself argues that he deserves mercy because his evil actions necessarily followed from the lack of compassion in his upbringing. As he tells Victor:

> I am malicious because I am miserable. Am I not shunned and hated by all mankind? You, my creator, would tear me to pieces, and triumph; remember that, and tell me why I should pity man more than he pities me? You would not call it murder if you could precipitate me into one of those ice-rifts, and destroy my frame, the work of your own hands. Shall I respect man when he contemns me? Let him live with me in the interchange of kindness; and, instead of injury, I would bestow every benefit upon him with tears of gratitude at his acceptance. But that cannot be; the human senses are insurmountable barriers to our union. Yet mine shall not be the submission of abject slavery. I will revenge my injuries: if I cannot inspire love, I will cause fear; and chiefly towards you my arch-enemy, because my creator, do I swear inextinguishable hatred. (125)

Clearly the question of nature versus nurture is a central issue in *Frankenstein*, with the creature arguing for nurture governing his character development and the creator arguing the being he created is innately evil.

That the issue remains unresolved in Mary Shelley's revision of the Pygmalion story is one of the chief elements that earmark it as Gothic; readers are presented with two irreconcilable points of view in Victor's and the creature's accounts; both argue plausibly, but to agree with one is to deny the other. While persuading Victor to make him a mate, the creature says: "My vices are the children of a forced solitude that I abhor; and my virtues will necessarily arise when I live in communion with an equal" (126–27). On the other hand, Victor believes the creature is evil and destroying it becomes his sole ambition:

> If I were engaged in any high undertaking or design, fraught with extensive utility to my fellow-creatures, then I could live to fulfill it. But such is not my destiny; I must pursue and destroy the being to whom I gave existence; then my lot on earth may be fulfilled, and I may die. (176)

In this bipolar relationship, Victor and the creature judge each other responsible for their unhappy lack of utility in the social world; both take responsibility only for ruining the other's life.

Dark Angel represents a third iteration of the Pygmalion/ Frankenstein story, one which recombines elements from the bucolic Pygmalion myth of social integration, with aspects of *Frankenstein*'s tragedy of social exclusion. In so doing, *Dark Angel* not only raises but answers the question of whether personal identity is innate or the result of learned behaviours, by demonstrating in Max an identity developed in the combination of those two precepts, an identity between the poles of the solipsistic self-interest of Frankenstein's creature and the total effacement by social role (wife and mother) of Pygmalion's statue.

The Dark Angel ≥ Frankenstein's Creature

The dark angel represents the uncanny as the term is understood by Sigmund Freud and exemplified by Frankenstein's creature. In his essay "The Uncanny," Freud observes:

> It often happens that male patients declare that they feel there is something uncanny about the female genital organs. This *unheimlich* place, however, is the entrance to the former *heim* [home] of all human beings, to the place where everyone dwelt once upon a time and in the beginning. (398–99)

Freud voices the belief, which he felt was commonly held in 1925, that even natural childbirth has uncanny conceptual implications. Like *Frankenstein*, *Dark Angel*'s narrative assumes that constructed (as opposed to procreated) humans are inherently uncanny. Unfortunately for the created beings of *Frankenstein* and *Dark Angel*, two uncanninesses don't cancel each other out; instead, their extra-vaginal origins mean that the creature and the dark angel suffer from uncanniness squared – they are intelligent beings conceived by intellect rather than intercourse, and as such deeply reflect long-standing anxieties over procreation and birth in general, and the artificial reproductive technologies in particular.

Repetition is a signature trait of the Gothic (Massé 2, Botting 177, DeLamotte 24), which operates in both *Frankenstein* and *Dark Angel*. Gothic repetition involves a claustrophobic recursion between two mutually exclusive premises. For example, the dark angel appears to be doomed to shuttle between the two poles of X5-452's repression in an authoritarian hierarchy, and Max's solipsistic independence as someone who was "just looking out for herself. No responsibilities, no entanglements" (Logan in "The Berrisford Agenda"). Repetition in *Dark Angel* involves iteration or, "recursive symmetries between different levels of the system" (169) as defined by N. Katherine Hayles in *Chaos Bound*. When Max makes choices, she learns; this iterative learning represents growth, particularly in her recognition of possibilities outside of those learned from her Manticore and Jam Pony years. Specifically, Tamy Burnett suggests in her unpublished dissertation, "'Just A Girl:' The Community-Centered Cult Television Heroine, 1995–2007," that Max's choices come to privilege community (148, 153) over regimentation or solipsism.

For example, in the pilot episode, Logan Cale and Max initially meet when Max attempts to burgle his apartment and steal a statue of the cat goddess Bast, whom she describes as "the goddess who comprehends all goddesses, eye of Ra, protector, avenger, and destroyer, giver of life, who lives forever," a coy homage to the character of Catwoman and private acknowledgement of Max's own feline genetic heritage. Max's spectacular escape causes Logan to suspect she is transgenic. He manages to find out where she lives and asks her help in protecting a woman named Lauren Braganza and her daughter Sophy. Braganza is a witness willing to expose a vicious corrupt city official, Edgar Sonrisa. Max refuses, saying that she's "more interested in going fast on my motorcycle or climbing the Trans American building with my pals." Without Max's help, Logan's project fails – in a shootout with Sonrisa's guards, Logan is permanently injured and Sophy is kidnapped. Sympathetic to the child because of her own past as a child fugitive, Max changes her mind – she manipulates Sonrisa's chief bodyguard into assassinating his boss while rescuing Sophy. Thus, Max's first decision – to stay uninvolved – is based on considerations of individual good and leaves her feeling badly; her second decision is based on considerations of social good and leaves her feeling better about herself. In this manner, she begins to develop a sense of social responsibility unlike anything she'd encountered either at Manticore or in her life on the street. When Max changes her mind is the exact moment when she grows, unlike Frankenstein's creature, who remains trapped by his claustrophobic recursive relationship with Victor Frankenstein.

The concept of iteration also describes X5-452's identity within Manticore. She is at risk of meeting a younger version of herself as happens in "...And Jesus Brought a Casserole," the final episode of season one. This X7 version of 452 is both a repetition, in that she is an exact copy X5-452, and an iteration, in that she will always be the younger of the two.

The dark angel's suffering further reinforces her as a Gothic heroine according to the precepts put forward by Michelle Massé in *In the Name of Love*, who states "it is a critical commonplace that the [Gothic] is 'about' suffering women whose painful initiations provide some vague pleasure for women authors, characters, and readers" (1). Certainly, Max's situation leads to suffering. For example, her variegated genetics get her into trouble sexually. The episode called "Heat," begins with her voice-over saying:

> I am in heat or something like that… All because they spiced up the genetic cocktail called me with a dash of feline DNA. So I can jump fifteen feet of razor wire and take out a 250-pound linebacker with my thumb and index finger, which makes me an awesome killing machine and a hoot at parties. But it also means that three times a year I'm climbing the walls looking for some action.

Later in "Heat," Max picks up a guy named Eric at Crash, the grunge club of choice on *Dark Angel*; when she gets him home, he's so drunk that he merely passes out on her bed. At the end of the episode, Eric asks, "the other night…was it as amazing for you as it was for me?" Max reassures him by saying, "Eric, you *the man*." More seriously, by the end of season one, she and Logan Cale have finally decided to commit to each other as a couple, but in the first episode of season two, "Designate This," she is infected by a virus designed by Manticore and targeted at Logan, with the sole function of infecting him with a deadly disease. They cannot touch each other, a fact that leads to many close-ups of her pensive, miserable face in subsequent episodes, as they try to let each other go, romantically. Whether played for laughter or for tears, Max's desires lead to the female suffering that Massé suggests is part of the perverse pleasure of the Gothic genre.

Max also fits Diane Long Hoeveler's exemplar model of Gothic heroines discussed in her book *Gothic Feminism: The Professionalization of Gender from Charlotte Smith to the Brontës*. According to Hoeveler, Gothic heroines "ostensibly appear to be conforming to acceptable roles within the patriarchy but… actually subvert the father's power at every possible occasion and then retreat to studied postures of conformity whenever they risk exposure to public censure" (6). In her need to hide her genetically enhanced abilities, Max falls neatly into the model of a woman who is "covertly powerful" (xvi) and still maintains "the illusion of the heroine's original identity as complaisant and malleable" (xvi). While undercover as a hooker in Sonrisa's mansion in the pilot episode, Max is thoroughly frisked by bodyguard Bruno Anselmo while Sonrisa looks on. In a classic example of dramatic irony, Max and the audience know full well that she is in control of the situation, but in the eyes of the male characters, Max is helpless, a misconception that she does nothing to dispel. This scene has a near parallel in the second season of *Buffy the Vampire Slayer*: in the episode "Phases," Buffy hides her strength from her classmates during a self-defence practice in gym class, although she still manages to trounce one sexist bully. Like Buffy's strength, Max's empowerment is palpable to watchers, though obscure to Anselmo and Sonrisa.

Thus, Max exhibits traits characteristic of a Gothic heroine in her identity as a fifth-generation genetic iteration of herself; in that her emotional pain is on display for the audience's viewing pleasure; and in her sometimes comic, sometimes tragic kowtowing to patriarchal hegemony. However, unlike Frankenstein's creature – trapped by his obsessive relationship with his creator, as denoted by the fact that he is known only as Frankenstein's creature – the dark angel has multiple sources of identity, and the potential for character growth.

The Dark Angel ≥ Pygmalion's Statue

The dark angel is also uncanny as that term is used by Bill Brown and illustrated by Pygmalion's statue. In his 1998 article "How to Do Things with Things (A Toy Story)," Brown refines Freud's use of "uncanny," described above, by putting it in the context of object theory. Brown observes that "when the subject-object relation is temporalized to the point of becoming recognizable as a negotiation, when the object appears to assume a life of its own, this is when we discover the uncanniness of everyday life" (939). In other words, when an object's presence prompts people to relate to it as if it had agency – the way Pygmalion treats his statue before it is animated – then that object has become uncanny. Nonetheless Brown limits his analysis to the untransformed object; Max, like Pygmalion's statue, is an animated construct, and so her subjectivity is no longer as tightly controlled as an inanimate object, however uncanny it may be.

Like "Pygmalion and the Statue," *Dark Angel* eventually becomes a story of social integration, but it explores the development of subjectivity and society for the created being, not the creator. Though she is neither wife nor mother, over the course of the first season Max compensates for the lack of compassionate nurturing in her own childhood by being fiercely protective of children and their parents, particularly mothers. This ethic of caring for family emerges from such minimal versions as a single scene in which Max berates a stranger contemplating suicide because he's letting his own misery occlude his responsibility for wife and child ("Art Attack") to the last four episodes of season one, wherein Max discovers that another of the X5 escapees, Tinga, has had a child. Manticore personnel actively hunt both mother and child, while Max and her allies work to protect and later avenge them. Thus the plot of protecting mothers and their children iterates through scenes, episodes and the entire first season. *Dark Angel's* preoccupation with protecting the mother-child bond resonates with the Pygmalion myth and also provides a community-based alternative to the binary which has heretofore governed Max's life – the repressive hierarchy of Manticore, and the solipsistic self-determination of her street existence in post-pulse Seattle.

Iteration provides a model for Max's extraordinary character development in the first season's episode "Pollo Loco," which begins with Max bringing home a live chicken for dinner. When Original Cindy expresses reservations about killing it, Max replies,

"Must be my feline DNA, 'cause when I look at this little face, I see dinner." Max then wrings the chicken's neck, off-camera: we hear the cracking and see Original Cindy's reaction. Original Cindy (an every-human figure in this episode) quickly gets over her squeamishness and approves of the execution once the bird is cooked. The short tale of the chicken's tragic fate foreshadows the main plot of the episode. Like Frankenstein's creature, X5-escapee Ben has become a serial murderer of humans which invites the paranoid progression: as chickens are to humans, so humans are to X5s. This simplistic structure is extended when, after various narrative twists, Max reluctantly becomes her brother's executioner, adding another layer to the progression: so other X5s are to Max. Ben's death is portrayed exactly like that of the chicken, with the camera not on the deed itself, but on Max's suffering face, which – as we have already learned from Massé – is the perverse focus of pleasure in a Gothic text. The iterated deaths in this episode escalate from chicken, to human/stranger, to X5/brother and parallel Max's iterated sense of self as feline, human and X5. Though she may have begun as a genetic construct just as Pygmalion's statue was an artistic construct, through actual and emotional experiences unanticipated by her Manticore makers, Max's identity grows far beyond the straightforward, obedient soldier 452 was intended to be.

Logan + Lydecker = Pygmalion

Massé suggests that another of the "formal characteristics of the Gothic [is the] alliance of horror and romance plot" (2). In *Dark Angel*, Donald Lydecker represents the repressive father of the Gothic horror plot while Logan Cale features as the permissive lover in the romance plot, thereby splitting the role of Pygmalion between them. The two appear to be irreconcilable for most of the first season.

Lydecker wants X5-452 to submit to military authority. Though he calls the escaped X5s "my kids" collectively ("Cold Comfort," "Meow"), the Manticore mastermind identifies individual escapees by the genetically encoded barcode numbers on the backs of their necks, indicating that he classes them as iterated units rather than individuals. Furthermore, Lydecker's name is a riff off of "Deckard" the hero of Philip K. Dick's *Do Androids Dream of Electric Sheep?*; Lydecker is like Deckard in that he hunts "made" beings, but unlike Deckard in that he is devious in his actions. He is a Lying Deckard.

In contrast, Logan represents the lover/husband aspect of Pygmalion; he knows the dark angel as Max Guevara, the name she chose for herself undoubtedly in homage to Che Guevara, the socialist/anarchist freedom fighter (Burnett 125, Jowett paragraph 35; in "Heat" Logan wears a T-shirt featuring a picture of the Cuban revolutionary). Where Lydecker expects unquestioning obedience from X5-452, Logan provides Max with information and trusts that she will decide on a course of action which will improve the post-apocalyptic social world in which they live.

In her article "Dr. Frankenstein Meets Dr. Freud," Maggie Kilgour points out that in a Gothic narrative any simple binary destabilizes, an observation upheld in the initially irreconcilable binary of Logan and Lydecker. They begin to interact late in season one, in "Pollo Loco," which is the eighteenth of twenty-two episodes. Because Max's decision to deal with the rogue X5, Ben, puts her in danger, Logan initiates a technology-mediated meeting with Lydecker in an attempt to enlist his aid. In a twisted echo of Pygmalion's prayer to Venus, each man petitions the other for help – Logan wants Manticore to stop Ben before Max is involved; Lydecker wants Logan to help him capture X5-452. The father figure listens to the lover's argument, then refutes it, pointing out that the X5s:

"were designed to kill. Coldly…efficiently…and happily. You think because she's so pretty she isn't as dangerous? They're all killers. All they need is a trigger. You may think you have some kind of relationship between the two of you, but let me tell you something, son; she's not the girl next door. You have no idea what she's capable of doing." ("Pollo Loco")

Later in the episode, Lydecker faxes Logan photos of a nine-year-old Max, smiling and drenched in blood after a murderous training exercise. Thus, where Pygmalion places himself in the goddess's power, Logan tries to manipulate Lydecker into recognizing Max's individuality, and Lydecker tries to manipulate Logan into recognizing Max as an iterated unit. Neither achieves his goal immediately; despite this potential for an alliance, the conflicting "prayers" of father and lover cancel each other out, and the divide between creator and lover remains until the season finale. But they do work together with Max in the doomed attack on Manticore in "…And Jesus Brought a Casserole," thus bringing together the horror (Lydecker) and romance (Logan) plots as Massé predicts.

The splitting of Pygmalion into Lydecker and Logan helps commute the incestuous connotations of the Pygmalion myth, in that the putative father is no longer the potential lover. Instead, *Dark Angel* flirts with a different incestuous relationship; Max's alpha X5 "brother" and fellow escapee Zack has more than a sibling's affection for her. At one point he compares Max with the other X5s, saying "It's different with you. I mean, how could I forget a single thing about you? How could I?" ("The Kidz are Aiight"). Then, in the season one finale, Zack literally gives his heart for Max. During the climatic melee, which they lose, Max is shot through the chest. Zach blows out his own brains to ensure that he is not captured by Manticore and that an X5 heart is available for her. Zack's character briefly returns as a cyborg in season two's "Some Assembly Required;" because his brain was damaged in his suicide/sacrifice, he cannot distinguish between false and real memories and briefly asserts that he and Max were lovers. She arranges for him to live far from her, where she cannot stimulate his memories with her presence. These sacrifices – Zack's self-sacrifice in season one, and Max's sacrifice of him in season two – serve the plot on several levels: they remove the incest complication from the narrative; they affirm the extraordinary loyalty that Max inspires; they clear the X5 hierarchy of its alpha, leaving an opening for a leader; they simplify the rivalry among Logan, Zack and Lydecker by removing one element; and finally, they exponentially increase Max's Gothic burden of female suffering.

Dark Angel ≠ *Buffy the Vampire Slayer* and/or *Twilight*

In *Dark Angel*, the ordinary humans' media-hyped fear of transgenics is a clear metaphor for the racial prejudices that inspire the civil rights movement, the gender biases that inspire affirmative action and the sexual preference prejudices that inspire gay pride activisms. One of the most vehemently anti-transgenic characters is Max's boss at Jam Pony Express: Reagan "Normal" Ronald. As much as possible, Normal abets the persecutors of Manticore's transgenics throughout both seasons. However, in "Freak Nation," the final episode of the series, he realizes that transgenics are no more inherently evil than any other minority. First he discovers that his friend Alec is an X5:

> NORMAL: My golden boy's a mutant.
> ALEC: We prefer "genetically empowered."
> NORMAL: Take me, Jesus.

Though Normal is taken aback by this revelation, it doesn't alter his opinion about transgenics significantly – he simply feels betrayed. This changes later in the episode; while trapped by a mob that wants to lynch the desperate transgenics, Normal helps deliver one of their children. Afterward, he is interviewed by a television reporter:

> REPORTER: Tell us about your captors. What are these creatures like? Is it true you delivered a transgenic baby?
> NORMAL: Yes, I did indeed. And a beautiful, bouncing baby girl she is.
> REPORTER: So you're saying they're not all monsters, then?
> NORMAL: Monsters? No. No more than you and me.

Normal's fear was created by a corrupt fifth estate, controlled by government and business; it dissipates when he realizes that many of the people who work for him are transgenic, driven into hiding by the fear mongered by the very media which fed his paranoia. In *Dark Angel*, moral action stems from individual decisions; social conventions are subject to external control via the media and are therefore not to be trusted.

One example of an approval of laissez-faire attitudes on the part of individuals arises when Max's friend and roommate Kendra moves in with the same corrupt cop who used to extort bribes from the girls ("Pilot," "Red"). Though she is puzzled by Kendra's choice of lover, Max doesn't judge her former roommate because of it. Similarly, Max bears no rancour when, in the middle of some delicate cat burgling, the fugitive Diamond cuts in to abscond with the boodle, leaving Max to the tender mercies of the police ("Shorties in Love"). Max, too, has done morally ambiguous things, not only during her childhood at Manticore, but also since her escape; in "Flushed," Max's rescue of a young orphan from an abusive prison warden is edited with flashbacks of a younger, newly escaped Max abandoning a similarly abused girl in her foster family. These examples demonstrate Dark Angel's insistently reiterated privileging of personal responsibility over conformation within social expectations.

Dark Angel makes more of an effort to depict diversity than the other popular culture narratives examined in this volume, with the possible exception of *Catwoman*. All the leads in *A.I.: Artificial Intelligence*, and in the first several seasons of *Buffy the Vampire Slayer* are white, middle-class suburbanites. There's a clear social Darwinism at work in the Twilight quartet, aligning the aristocratic white vampires with intellect, wealth and expensive sports cars, and the Quileute shape-shifters with nature, emotion, substandard housing and broken-down vehicles (Wilson 55). *Dark Angel* avoids such reductiveness; its cast includes people from a variety of racial backgrounds, playing characters of varied religious, political and sexual orientations.

Dark Angel's championing of hybridity, symbolized by the plot's focus on transgenics and played out in the relative diversity of its characters, ensured that reviewers could not resist describing the show as recombined elements from previous screen fictions; *USA Today* called it "a sort of *Blade Runner* meets *Buffy the Vampire Slayer* on the set of *The X-Files*" (8/11/00, quoted in Dark Angel Media Quotes). That Max is, well, dark is a detail that reviewers loved to exploit; my favourite description came from *Time Out New York*, which suggested that you

> start with all three of Charlie's angels, and mix. Spoon in Wonder Woman's might. Add a dash of Jaime Sommers' bionic-ness, and whisk. Then, gently fold in Scully's smarts. Stir in copious amounts of Buffy's sass. Now pour in just a touch of Xena's brawn (not too much!). Dust lightly with Felicity's determination. Baste with Daisy Duke's sex appeal, and bake until golden brown. Voila! Meet Max, the ultimate TV heroine. (Emmanuel)

Some of *Dark Angel's* characters follow conventional unconventionality, so to speak, such as Herbal Thought, a black Rastafarian. Others are simply part of the story; Max's best friend, Original

Cindy, is black and lesbian and frequently plays the part of the every-human, a synecdochic signifier for the entire ordinary human population.

Nevertheless, *Dark Angel* does demonize one population: white men – a sadly predictable narrative counter to the first season's ethic of protection for women and children. Although the show includes a number of sympathetic straight Caucasian male characters like Logan and Zack, the WASPy Lydecker provides a typical visual profile of *Dark Angel* antagonists, such as: Normal; the first episode's Edgar Sonrisa; his hit man Bruno Anselmo; the prison warden of "Flushed"; Johanssen of "Red" and "Rising"; Gerhardt Bronck of "Out"; and even the mad X5 Ben of "Pollo Loco." Then, in the last third of the first season, in strides Lydecker's putative boss, Madame X to confuse the gender, if not the race, structure in place in *Dark Angel*. Her smiling perfidy renders the unthinkable – an alliance of Max and Logan with Lydecker – not only thinkable, but necessary. Even considered collectively, the male antagonists listed above pale before Madame X's pure self-interest. The men are portrayed with human traits that elicit sympathy from the audience, like Anselmo's love for his daughter ("Red"), and Lydecker's admission that he cares more for Max than for any other X5 – he included some of his dead wife's DNA in her cocktail, making her something of a stepdaughter to him ("...And Jesus Brought a Casserole").

In contrast, Madame X's treachery is comic book perfect. The carefully nurtured tenet that because all characters are motivated by varying degrees of self-interest and altruism their positions as protagonists or antagonists are mutable, breaks down before Madame X, whose evil is absolute in season one. In season two, Madame X gets a new name – Dr. Elizabeth Renfro, an allusion to Count Dracula's mad henchman, Renfield, in Bram Stoker's *Dracula*. For the first and most of the second episodes ("Designate This" and "Bag 'Em"), Renfro maintains her perfidious character by torturing X5-452 physically and mentally until she adopts postures of submission. Then at the end of "Bag 'Em" Renfro throws herself in front of 452, who is about to be gunned down by an assailant. Renfro dies before she can explain why she committed such an uncharacteristically selfless act.

Doctor Renfro is replaced by another affluent white man, Ames White, as the main antagonist of season two: the culmination of a five-millennia-long breeding program, White murders ordinary people without compunction, but loves his family beyond reason. The sympathetic details provided about Max's enemies throughout the show's run demonstrates how *Dark Angel* goes to great lengths to show that no character or population is inherently evil or good, though Ames White comes close; his love for his wife doesn't stop him from killing her. Rather than depending on reified good and bad guys, *Dark Angel* explores shifting allegiances among people motivated by differing measures of altruism and self-interest, compassion and fear.

Along with presenting an unusually wide mix of races, sexual orientations and lifestyle choices, *Dark Angel* also depicts people of varying physical abilities, most obviously in the case of Logan Cale. Logan receives a spinal cord injury in the pilot, and spends much of the rest of the first season in a wheelchair, a development with several symbolic functions. On one hand, his inability to walk provides a heightened comparison to Max's superabilities. On the other hand, Max suffers from less obvious health problems, such as intense sexual urges, seizures and the potential for premature aging ("Haven"), all of which are by-products of her spliced-together genetics. So, where Max is overtly hyper-enabled and insidiously disabled, Logan is overtly disabled, but nonetheless extremely competent intellectually and physically resourceful. For example, in "Haven," when Max succumbs to seizures, Logan fights off several men attacking their cottage through the intelligent use of various subterfuges and traps. The contrasting physical capacities of Max and Logan deliberately provoke questions about social definitions of disability, in a way that Max and Cindy's prominence question prejudices based on gender, race and sexual orientation.

That Logan is paraplegic works not only as a contrast to Max's genetic enhancements, but also emphasizes his intellectual altruism in the face of a corrupt society, which contrasts Max's responses to the same stimuli. Logan exposes the corruption of those in power simply because he feels that he must ("Pilot," "Red"). Max consistently resists taking on Logan's projects until she is compelled by empathy with the victims of corruption. In the pilot, Max refuses to help until Sophy is kidnapped; in "Out," Max resents that Logan interrupts a dinner date in order to stop an illegal shipment of unknown contraband, but when she discovers that the shipment includes kidnapped girls, she becomes completely engaged; in "Haven," she reacts with outrage when she discovers that Logan's idea of a weekend holiday includes research, but she colludes with him when a child's welfare becomes involved. Thus, though Logan and Max frequently act in concert and with a similar goal of defending diversity from a corrupt and largely white male power structure, Logan acts primarily from intellectual altruism, while Max acts primarily out of emotional compassion.

Dark Angel's (Max's [X5-452's Fall] Rise) Flattened Aspect

Unfortunately, *Dark Angel*'s graphic visual style undermines Max's developing identity. Virtually every scene elicits comparison with the framed aesthetic of an old-style comic book. The major characters pose in stances and with expressions that become signature aspects, thereby flattening them into facsimiles rather than believable personalities. The high-contrast lighting and teeming crowd scenes add false romanticism to Max's marginal existence; her home is a squat on the seventh floor of an abandoned apartment building unburdened by windows or utilities except, oddly, water. This portrayal of post-apocalyptic life bears witness to the Gothicism of *Dark Angel*'s narrative. The show's half-destroyed Seattle fits Alexandra Warwick's definition of urban Gothic from *The Handbook to Gothic Literature*, in which "the city is…a place of ruins, paradoxically always new but always decaying, a state of death-in-life" (289).

Not even Max's respect for the mother-child bond results in her integration into society by the end of season one. Instead, in the final episode, Max loses a fight to an X7 version of herself, reinscribing both Gothic tropes of iteration and the suffering woman. Furthermore, the kind of truncated "happily ever after" ending which Massé says earmarks Gothic fictions (2) is initially given then taken away to reveal a trap. Season one ends with a seamless fantasy sequence of the triumph of Max and her allies, which disintegrates when Logan embraces her and discovers blood on his hands. From a resolution of victory and celebration, viewers are wrenched back to the scene of battle, Max's apparent death and, finally, her actual imprisonment in the very place she most hoped to avoid: the bowels of Manticore.

Synthesis

Despite the darkness at the end of season one of *Dark Angel*, the show's status as a twenty-first century iteration of *Frankenstein*, itself a nineteenth century iteration of Ovid's first century Pygmalion myth, results in implications that offer hope for change and growth. Ovid's short tale has only enough space to state the fact of Pygmalion's social integration as husband of his statue and parent of the statue's child; the statue's subjectivity is not relevant enough to merit comment. In contrast, the novel *Frankenstein* thoroughly explores how Victor Frankenstein's social ostracism comes as a result of the scientist's hubris in wanting to father a new race of intelligent beings without undertaking the significant work of parenting. Like Pygmalion's statue, Victor Frankenstein's creature expedites his creator's fate; because their primary functions are as agents of destiny, neither statue nor creature is named, though the subjectivity of the creature is explored in the long passage of the novel which he narrates.

In contrast to the nameless statue and creature, the dark angel has two names, one for each character in the television show who, together, serve the narrative functions of Pygmalion. The repressive father-creator Colonel Donald Lydecker calls her by the number encoded in her DNA: X5-452. The permissive lover-creator Logan Cale calls her the name she chose for herself: Max Guevara. Max spent nearly all the first decade of her life defined by the military hierarchy which both created and indoctrinated her, and nearly all the second decade of her life reacting against the earlier identity by becoming a self-serving solipsist who acts only for her own advancement.

The irreducible binary represented by these two identities begins to change after she meets Logan; he encourages her to recognize a third possibility based on a sense of social compassion, in a wide social milieu that includes people of various races, genders and sexual orientations. In the first season, Max becomes a champion on a small scale, for the people whose causes she and Logan undertake. In the second season, she becomes a saviour for all the artificially gene-spliced creations of Manticore. In so doing, her two identities come close to integration – in negotiation with a detective in "Freak Nation," she first identifies herself as 452, then later tells him to call her Max. According to producer Charles H. Eglee, in the unmade third season, Max would have become the saviour for all intelligent life, whether their genes were spliced in a laboratory or in a womb (commentary from "Freak Nation").

Thus *Dark Angel* builds beyond the blankness of Pygmalion's statue – which served to integrate the sculptor into his social world – to depict a created being with subjectivity and character. *Dark Angel* also expands beyond the reified polarity of Victor Frankenstein who argued that his creation was inherently evil and

Frankenstein's creature who argued that nurture corrupted his potential; the dark angel's identity encompasses the hard-wired genetics of X5-452 and the learned experiences of Max Guevara to integrate both her dark and her angelic traits such that she is not just socially integrated but becomes a honourable leader in a largely corrupt society.

5.

THE TWILIGHT QUARTET:

Romance, Porn, Pain and Complicity

A few years ago, I walked into a Price Club and nearly fell over a jumbo pallet full of copies of *Breaking Dawn*, the final volume of Stephenie Meyer's quartet of young adult novels – *Twilight*, *New Moon*, *Eclipse* and *Breaking Dawn*. It was a solid pile of books about two metres square, stacked higher than my waist. Thousands upon thousands of copies. Hardcover. The density of the stack rivalled that of the trees which died to bring it into being. And I thought to myself "there are similar piles in similar warehouse stores all over North America, not to say smaller batches in actual bookstores." None could afford not to stock it.

The logistics implied by that block of books boggled my brain: whole effluent ponds of inks and glues; hectare upon hectare of clear-cuts worth of paper. How much fuel had been burnt in how many boats/trains/trucks just getting the raw materials to the printing presses, let alone transporting the finished books to the stores? How much plastic and how many heavy metals in all the computers and readers used to both create and access the texts? Think of the retail managers, from head office VPs down to aisle supervisors, calculating each book as a unit of sale, no different than the bags of fertilizer I was actually searching for that day. To say nothing of the movies and related spinoffs: posters, bookbags, key chains and so on.

That pallet of books in Price Club was tangible, local proof of the kind of commodification that Marianne Martens discusses in her article "Consumed by Twilight: The Commodification of Young Adult Literature": "Conglomeration has created a marketplace in which commodified transmedia products that can potentially generate profits on multiple platforms, such as domestic books, foreign editions, films, and licensed merchandise, are valued higher than innovative and creative works of high literary merit (Jenkins, 2006)" (243).

The 2,444 page Twilight quartet of novels (*Twilight* = 498 pages, *New Moon* = 563, *Eclipse* = 629 and *Breaking Dawn* = 754) is narrated almost entirely by protagonist Isabella Swan, a high school student who prefers to be called "Bella" (*Twilight* 44; throughout this essay, *Twilight* in italics denotes the first book while Twilight in regular text denotes the entire quartet). Like the real Arabella Fermor who became "Belle" in Pope's "Rape of the Lock," the fictional Isabella Marie Swan embraces a nickname of diminution and objectification (*Twilight* 16, 25, 44).

The plot begins with Bella's move away from her mother, Renée, in Phoenix to her father's household in rainy Forks, Oregon. Renée has remarried and so Bella decides to absent herself rather than impede the new relationship (*Twilight* 49); this is the first of many self-sacrifices on Bella's part. The novels follow Bella's increasingly consuming love for Edward Cullen, the handsome youngest son of the town's foremost surgeon, and, by the way, a vampire – but that's all right because his adoptive family of vampires, the Cullens, are "vegetarians" (188). They have made the difficult ethical choice to survive on animal, not human, blood. One consequence of the Cullens' unusual diet is that their eyes are golden, rather than the red of human-consuming vampires in Twilight. In further departures from vampire traditions, some of Twilight's vampires have extrasensory capacities, such as Edward's clairvoyance, and all are made of what amounts to diamond, which means they are extremely durable, animated statues who find humans very fragile in comparison. Twilight's vampires outshine Pygmalion's sculpture; they're not only preternaturally beautiful, but also glitter like faceted stones in sunlight.

The literary merit of the Twilight quartet is much debated. On the one hand, the books are celebrated among readers and scholars like Amy M. Clarke, Margaret M. Toscano, Philip Puszczalowski and Marc E. Shaw. In terms of writing craft, Meyer's plots compel; the characters are strong and consistent, and their actions are plausible. Her style makes me wince, but it has garnered her wealth and celebrity; why ever would she change it? The books evince a wry humour almost completely missing from the movies, and the revision of vampire mythology is both internally consistent and highly imaginative. Allusions to prior texts like *Romeo and Juliet*, *Pride and Prejudice* and *Wuthering Heights* are deft, if sometimes obvious (see Kisor). Meyer models the antagonistic relationship between vampires and the shape-shifters on that of Shakespeare's Montagues and Capulets (*New Moon* 11, 17, 369–70, 426–27, 452, 552, 555; *Eclipse* 28). Nevertheless, the ways they are able to eventually set aside their differences and work together adroitly departs from Shakespeare's original. The books explore issues of free will versus compulsion in the context of social responsibility: the "vegetarian" Cullens contrast the aristocratic Volturi vampires; Jacob's determination to do what he thinks is right contrasts his biological imperative to obey the pack's alpha, Sam (see Toscano 26, 27). As far as creating an entertaining, thought-provoking narrative goes, Meyer does many things quite well.

On the other hand, the texts' many problems are vociferously rehearsed online and in the academic presses. Technically, the quartet takes a critical beating for its limited and repetitive language use, as Sheffield and Merlo note in "Biting Back: Twilight Anti-Fandom and the Rhetoric of Superiority": "One reader on the Twilight Sucks! forum counted the number of times the words 'chagrin,' 'russet,' and 'grimace' appear in the four books (15, 25, and 71 respectively)" (212). I find the repetition of ideas even more tedious than that of vocabulary; many of the references in this essay include multiple pages over several volumes for a single, established trope such as the allusions to *Romeo and Juliet* noted above.

In terms of content, the Twilight narratives suffer from flaws both blatant and subtle. A friend spontaneously declared to me that Edward is a stalker because of the way he sleep-watches the oblivious Bella in *Twilight* – a term used by the police for this specific type of voyeurism – and Jacob is a pedophile for his imprinting on Edward and Bella's child Renesmee in *Breaking Dawn* (see also Clarke "Intro" 12 notes 12 and 14; and Housel 177–78). In her article "Bite Me! (Or Don't)," Christine Seifert coined the term "abstinence porn" to describe how, in Twilight, "sex is dangerous and men must control themselves. It's a matter of life or death, and ultimately men are in charge" (see also articles by Collins and Carmody, Platt, and Hawes for further criticism of gender relations in the novels, and Jeffers for a more positive take).

Less obvious are the problems explored in Kathryn Kane's article "A Very Queer Refusal: The Chilling Effect of the Cullens' Heteronormative Embrace." Kane discusses the novels' conservative revamping of vampire mythology to exclude all but the most heterosexual attributes, no mean feat given the gender-bending usually denoted by vampires with their "penetrating" mouths. By focusing on the Cullens' golden eyes, rather than their red lips, Meyer reclaims the vampire for heteronormativity (Kane 107). In "Civilized Vampires Versus Savage Werewolves: Race and Ethnicity in the Twilight Series," Natalie Wilson explores the books' racist underpinnings, which "associate whiteness with civility, beauty, and intellect on the one hand, and indigenous people with animality and primitivism on the other" (55; see also Jensen). Furthermore, in the Twilight novels, the dominance of patriarchy remains intact and unchallenged, as McClimans and Wisnewski observe in "Undead Patriarchy and the Possibility of Love." Clearly, the Twilight quartet taps into Western culture's current zeitgeist in unprecedentedly multifarious and controversial manners.

In a world rife with the detritus of marketing failures, the investment in the Twilight quartet of novels and associated transmedia could not have been so outrageously successful if the books didn't somehow promise to satisfy some collective, unslaked thirst felt by the individuals who read them: "The phenomenal sales of the Twilight series, and the fervor of the fans, suggests that the series fills an important void in some girls' and womens' lives" (Behm-Morawitz, Click and Aubrey 152; see also Kokkola). And therein lies the difference between composted sheep manure and books. One is for growing vegetables, the other for growing minds. Just what kind of growth the Twilight books encourage is an issue that engages reviewers, fan bloggers and scholars. Jennifer Stevens Aubrey, Scott Walus and Melissa A. Click note in "Twilight and the Production of the 21st Century Teen Idol" that "the core demographic of the franchise is young females" (230). Behm-Morawitz, Click and Aubrey further observe that these readers learn "about boys' thoughts about love, rules for showing affection, and sexual intercourse techniques from the books. Thus, for teen readers, romance novels provide a source of comparison that girls can use to judge their current and future relationships" (141; see also Clasen 131). Although the Twilight novels succeed as entertainment, their potential for creating unrealistic relational expectations is gravely problematic.

First Quarter: Romance

> Happiness. It made the whole dying thing pretty bearable.
>
> – Stephenie Meyer, *New Moon*

Bella as Romance Heroine

A romance novel is "a work of prose fiction that tells the story of the courtship and betrothal of one or more heroines" (Regis 14). Stephenie Meyer, "like many modern romance writers, argues for the empowerment of her heroine" (Hendershot Parkin 66) on the grounds that Bella Swan has agency, proven through the many choices she makes to determine her future (68; see also Jeffers). However, the analysis of the Harlequin Romances of the 1970s in Ann Barr Snitow's article "Mass Market Romance: Pornography for Women is Different" applies remarkably aptly to the Twilight novels, suggesting that Bella's story is a throwback to a bygone style of mass-market romance, one concerned primarily with the heroine's "bondage in love" (Regis xiii).

Early in her article, Snitow asserts that the Harlequin heroine's "most marketable virtue is her blandness" (251). The initial description of Bella Swan – just prior to boarding a plane that will take her from her home in Phoenix, Arizona – uses negative constructions that embody self-deprecation:

> Physically, I'd never fit in anywhere. I *should* be tan, sporty, blond – a volley-ball player, or a cheerleader, perhaps – all the things that go with living in the valley of the sun.
>
> Instead, I was ivory-skinned, without even the excuse of blue eyes or red hair, despite the constant sunshine. I had

always been slender but soft somehow, obviously not an athlete; I didn't have the necessary hand-eye coordination to play sports without humiliating myself – and harming both myself and anyone else who stood too close. (*Twilight* 10)

Bella Swan is white and flat – a blank page upon which readers can impose their fantasies.

Along with being blandly ordinary, a good mass-market romance heroine must "perform well in a number of female helping roles" demonstrating "passionate motherliness, good cooking, patience in adversity, efficient planning, and a good clothes sense" (Snitow 249). Bella is an exemplar of all of these traits. In this first book of the quartet, she nurtures both of her parents, describing Renée as "childlike" (*Twilight* 4), and telling Edward, "'My mom always says I was born thirty-five years old and that I get more middle-aged every year.' I laughed, and then sighed. 'Well, someone has to be the adult'" (106). Bella's father, Charlie, tells her "You baby me too much" (358), as she jumps up from the meal that she just cooked for him in order to do the dishes. This brings us to one of the first things Bella does when she moves in with her father: "I requested that I be assigned kitchen detail for the duration of my stay. He was willing enough to hand over the keys to the banquet hall" (*Twilight* 31). Thereafter the first book is peppered with references to her culinary prowess (33, 35, 37, 78, etc.). When she is responsible for her own nutrition, she eats cold cereal or leftovers (54, 315, etc.), or skips meals entirely (40, 86, etc.); she cooks only for Charlie and his friends (35, 78, 237–38, etc.).

As Snitow prescribes, Bella is patient in adversity. For example, Bella first meets Edward when they are partnered in a biology class at school. He spurns her for no apparent reason – it isn't until later in the first volume that we find out that the smell of her blood is so attractive to him that he describes her as "exactly my brand of heroin" (*Twilight* 268). In any case, she decides – while cooking chicken enchiladas ("a long process, and it would keep me busy" [*Twilight* 78]) – "I could leave him alone. I would leave him alone. I would get through my self-imposed sentence here in purgatory, and then hopefully some school in the Southwest, or possibly Hawaii, would offer me a scholarship" (79), indicating her ability to delay gratification in adverse circumstances.

Bella also demonstrates the requisite "good clothes sense" predicted by Snitow (249). Though she cannot afford designer clothes, she admires them on Edward and the rest of his family (*Twilight* 487). But when they give such clothing to her, Bella's romance-heroine-appropriate blandness ensures she is not comfortable wearing them. For example, she accuses Edward's sister Alice of treating her like "Guinea Pig Barbie" because Alice dressed her in "the most ridiculous dress – deep blue, frilly and off the shoulders, with French tags" (482) in preparation for attending Edward's prom. She does, however, demonstrate excellent taste, even though she can't afford designer fashions. While preparing to spend a day with Edward, Bella describes how she dressed in a white shirt, tan sweater and jeans (252). That this conservative chic is exactly correct is evident by Edward's similar clothing: as they meet, he chuckles and then says, "'We match.' He laughed again. I realized he had a long, light tan sweater on, with a white collar showing underneath, and blue jeans" (253; see also 5, 170, 318, etc.).

Bella is also very good at planning. For example, near the end of *Twilight*, Charlie is unknowingly imperilled because of Bella's proximity to Edward and his family. A conventional vampire named James has decided to hunt Bella for the sport of spiting the Cullen clan (397). In this emergency, neither Edward nor his sibling Emmett extemporize the best plan to protect him. It is Bella who suggests:

> "You take me back. I tell my dad I want to go home to
> Phoenix. I pack my bags. We wait till [James] is watching, and

then we run. He'll follow us and leave Charlie alone. Charlie won't call the FBI on your family. Then you can take me any damned place you want."

They stared at me, stunned.

"It's not a bad idea, really." Emmett's surprise was definitely an insult. (384)

Nor does Bella depend on the Cullens to execute her plans; while Edward is off chasing a false trail, James tricks Bella into thinking that he has kidnapped her mother and will kill her if Bella doesn't come to him alone. Bella plans and then successfully executes her plan to escape from Edward's other siblings Alice and Jasper (440), despite Jasper's supernatural empathic powers and Alice's supernatural precognition.

It is Bella's impressive facility at prevarication which demonstrates that, of all the traits of a good romance heroine, the ability to lie is the one she most clearly embodies. Snitow observes that the heroine "lies constantly to hide her desires, to protect her reputation" (251). In the first book alone, Bella says:

> "I *want* to go," I lied. (4)
> I can do this, I lied to myself feebly. (14)
> Mostly I just lied a lot. (17)
> "Fine," I lied. (28)
> "Nope," I lied lightly. (114)
> "No," I lied. (224)
> "No." I tried to make the lie sound confident. (254)
> I lied again. (254)
> "I don't find you scary at all, actually," I lied casually. (345)
> "I'm fine," I lied. (477)

The first four examples concern Bella hiding her desire to leave Forks from the people who live there. Then she meets Edward; in the next, she is protecting her reputation by hiding her desire for him from her peers (114). In the final five she hides from

Edward himself the fear he inspires in her, evenly compounded of anxiety over appearing foolish in front of him (254, twice), fear of abandonment by him (477) and direct fear of his potential for the violent predation that stands in for sexuality in these novels (224, 345). (Bella lies by omission and in her actions as well. See 38, 60, 122, 190, 213, 226, 249, 251, 296, 394, 427, etc.)

Bland?
    Check.
Maternal?
    Check.
Good cook?
    Check.
Patient in adversity?
    Check.
Conservative, thrifty dresser?
    Check.
Good emergency planner?
    Check.
Liar?
    Check.

If that list seems a trifle tedious, if her fashion sense seems more grave than haute, that is to be expected of a mass-market romance heroine. After all, "for women, being ordinary and being attractive are equated in these novels. Heroes are of course expected to have a little more dash and sometimes sports cars" (Snitow 251).

Edward as Romance Hero

Aubrey observes that "Edward certainly serves as the hero archetype of the romance genre" (226). He has the advantage of being male, which, in the world of the mass-market romance, makes him synonymous with active, exciting and mysterious; the hero of

1970s Harlequin novels is "a sexual icon whose magic is maleness. The books are permeated by phallic worship. Male is good, male is exciting, without further points of reference. Cruelty, callousness, coldness, menace, etc. are all equated with maleness and treated as a necessary part of the package" (Snitow 248). Being the male hero also means being dangerous, particularly to a heroine who is, to paraphrase the Rodgers and Hammerstein song, "just getting to know" him…

> Edward Cullen's back stiffened, and he turned slowly to glare at me – his face was absurdly handsome – with piercing, hate-filled eyes. For an instant, I felt a thrill of genuine fear, raising the hair on my arms. (*Twilight* 27; see also pages 42, 54, 64)

…getting to know all about him…

> He *was* dangerous. He'd been trying to tell me that all along. (93; see also pages 65, 92, 107, 190, 266)

…because she's getting to like him…

> I felt a spasm of fear at his words, and the abrupt memory of his violent black glare that first day … but the overwhelming sense of safety I felt in his presence stifled it. (175)

… and getting to hope that he likes her too.…

> About three things I was absolutely positive. First, Edward was a vampire. Second, there was part of him – and I didn't know how potent that part might be – that thirsted for my blood. And third, I was unconditionally and irrevocably in love with him. (195; this quote also appears on the back cover of *Twilight*, with the word "potent" replaced by "dominant.")

Thus bland Bella's attraction to glamorous, dangerous Edward fulfills the genre conventions of the 1970s mass-market romance.

Along with a hero marked by "cruelty, callousness, coldness, menace" (Snitow 248), in 1970s mass-market romances "the hero is always quite a bit older than the heroine" (251). Edward was born in 1901 and "turned" in 1918 (*Twilight* 287). He is a centenarian teenager, a fact which causes Bella no small distress: "I was getting closer to nineteen every stinking day, while Edward stayed frozen in all his seventeen-year-old perfection, as he had for over ninety years" (*Breaking Dawn* 16; see also *Twilight* 185, 476; *New Moon* 7; *Eclipse* 119). Thus, in the case of Edward, the mass-market romance hero's authority of seniority is balanced by his youthful good looks.

Edward's beauty is a requisite aspect of the romance hero's objectification by the heroine:

Since all action in the novels is described from the female point of view… (Snitow 247)

Of course he wasn't interested in me, I thought angrily, my eyes stinging – a delayed reaction to the onions. (*Twilight* 79)

…the reader identifies with the heroine's efforts to decode the erratic gestures of "tall, dark and gravely handsome" men, all mysterious strangers or powerful bosses…. (Snitow 247– 48)

I wasn't *interesting*. And he was. (*Twilight* 79)

In a sense the usual relationship is reversed: the woman is subject, man, object. (Snitow 248)

> Interesting…and brilliant…and mysterious…and
> perfect…and beautiful…and possibly able to lift full-size
> vans with one hand. (*Twilight* 79)

One aspect of the hero's objectification is the plethora of descriptions of him: Snitow's prediction that there will be "more descriptions of his body than hers" (248) is played out in *Twilight*. Bella makes repeated observations about Edward: "he looked like he'd just finished shooting a commercial for hair gel" (43), "I couldn't imagine how an angel could be any more glorious" (241), and "There was no way this godlike creature could be meant for me" (256; see also 19, 65, 262, 292, 311, 358, 452). In this situation, the mass-market romance genre inverts conventional gender expectations exemplified by Pygmalion's objectification of his beloved statue. It is the male hero, Edward, who is objectified in the author's, heroine's and readers' minds, because the books are written from the heroine's point of view; his physical self is described frequently and with superlatives. Edward also has the requisite sports car, an Aston Martin Vanquish (*Breaking Dawn* 329) – previous to Twilight, a vehicle most famous for being the vehicle driven by James Bond in *Die Another Day*.

Thus, Edward has the cruelty, callousness, coldness, menace, age, damned good looks and car, while Bella has the blandness, mother-wit, ability to cook, patience-in-adversity, efficiency-in-planning, good clothes sense and facility for lying required for the hero and heroine of a 1970s mass-market romance.

Second Quarter: Porn

> I'd forgotten what real happiness felt like.
> Happiness. It made the whole dying thing pretty bearable.
>
> – Stephenie Meyer, *New Moon*

Sex and the Twilight Quartet

In the previous section, I took advantage of Snitow's veritable grocery list of traits defining the heroine and hero of a 1970s mass-market romance; that list is the most superficial aspect of her article's analysis. Snitow also provides a comprehensive critique of ways in which mass-market romances are pornography designed specifically for women:

> In a sexist society, we have two pornographies, one for men, one for women. They both have, hiding within them, those basic human expressions of abandon…. The pornography for men enacts this abandon on women as objects. How different is the pornography for women, in which sex is bathed in romance, diffused, always implied rather than enacted at all? (257; see also Wagner.)

The trust required for a woman to enact abandon does not come easily. Consequently, Snitow asserts, the heroine has to find a hero whose offer of marriage indicates that he has committed to multiple sexual encounters, so that she can learn how to have as much libidinal fun as he: "A one-night stand won't work; she is only just beginning to get her emotional generators going when he is already gone. And orgasm? It probably hasn't happened" (258).

According to Snitow, this is one reason why, in a traditional mass-market romance, sex cannot happen until marriage: "The hero wants sex; the heroine wants it too, but can only enjoy it after the love promise has finally been made and the ring is on her finger" (254).

The heroine "must somehow teach the hero to take time, to pay attention, to feel, while herself remaining passive, undemanding, unthreatening" (260), a difficult task, since she herself is largely ignorant of her own desires, let alone how to fulfill them (258). In the Twilight series, most of the scenes wherein Bella tries to talk about sex go on for pages without using that one, little, three-letter word (*Twilight* 309–11, *Eclipse* 435–55, *Breaking Dawn* 65–69); in fact, "sex" shows up only six times in the 2,444 published pages of the quartet (*Eclipse* 58, 61, and on 235 twice, as the adjective "sexy"; *Breaking Dawn* 99, 11). Far from knowing what she needs in order to express herself, Bella is at a loss, sexually.

According to Snitow, there are four stages to the process of learning to fulfill the romance heroine's sexual needs. In the first stage, "the man is hard (a walking phallus)" (Snitow 260). This is certainly true of Edward. The first time he touches Bella with intent, he uses his hardness to save her from being crushed in the school parking lot: "Just before I heard the shattering crunch of the van folding around the truck bed, something hit me, hard, but not from the direction I was expecting. My head cracked against the icy blacktop, and I felt something solid and cold pinning me to the ground" (*Twilight* 56). That "something solid and cold" is Edward.

In Snitow's second stage, the heroine realizes she "likes this hardness" (Snitow 260). When Edward first kisses her, Bella's autonomic reaction surprises them both:

And then his cold, marble lips pressed very softly against mine.

What neither of us was prepared for was my response.

Blood boiled under my skin, burned in my lips. My breath came in a wild gasp. My fingers knotted in his hair, clutching him to me. My lips parted as I breathed in his heady scent. (*Twilight* 282)

Bella's uninhibited reaction causes Edward to "turn to unresponsive stone," although "his eyes were wild" (282), as he struggles to maintain self-control. As Snitow predicts, she likes his hardness – so much so, it nearly causes him to kill her.

In the third step, the lovers-to-be admit the obstacles that must be overcome to enable satisfying sex; "at the outset, this hardness is too hard" (Snitow 260). When Bella asks Edward if they could ever be intimate, he is appalled at the thought, because, as he tells her, "I could reach out, meaning to touch your face, and crush your skull by mistake. You don't realize how incredibly *breakable* you are. I can never, never afford to lose any kind of control when I'm with you" (*Twilight* 310). Edward's statement indicates how the Twilight novels invert the Pygmalion myth. Edward is an animated statue, the beloved object. He is also the patriarchal agent, reluctantly engaged in a drawn-out process of making Bella over in his image.

In the fourth and final stage for achieving sexual pleasure for a mass-market romance heroine, Snitow avers that "her final release of sexual feeling depends on his changing his mind, but not too much. He must become softer…but not too soft. For good sex, he must be hard but this hardness must be at the service of the woman" (260). In the Twilight quartet, however, it is not Edward who becomes softer; the only way for Bella to tolerate his hardness is to become equally hard. The process by which Bella becomes a vampire is a convoluted negotiation centred on Bella's virginity. (Though Edward is also a virgin, neither Bella nor he expresses much compunction about relieving him of his inexperience [*Twilight* 311].)

Initially, in *Twilight*, Bella survives Edward's hardness through his monumental forbearance. When Bella and Edward begin discussions in earnest in *New Moon*, she already has the promise of Edward's sire, Carlisle, patriarch of the Cullens, to change her into a vampire. She wants Edward to do the deed, which gives him a strong position from which to negotiate (538–39). Edward proposes that she wait five years; they barter about the time period briefly but fail to compromise. Edward changes tactics and proposes… literally: he will change Bella if she agrees to marry him and so hedge their moral and mortal bets (540). Though the shambles of her parents' failed marriage has prejudiced Bella against early marriage, she is more tempted by Edward's offer than she is willing to let on: "Now that I knew there was a chance that Edward would change me himself, I wanted it bad" (542).

Nearly five hundred pages later, Bella comes up with a counter and offers to marry Edward if he will attempt to have sex with her while she's still human, so that she can enjoy it before the blood lust of a young vampire overwhelms her (*Eclipse* 446). Edward still fears the harm he could cause Bella in the throes of lovemaking – "'No,' he murmured silkily. 'It's not possible now. Later, when you're less breakable. Be patient, Bella'" (446). For most of *Eclipse*, Edward protects Bella's virtue (read: virginity) from her intention to have premarital sex with him, causing Bella to observe that Edward is "bizarrely moral for a vampire" (*Eclipse* 536). At the end of *Eclipse*, though, she has worn him down enough to counter her counter, agreeing to attempt sex before she is changed, but only after they are married, a proposition to which she agrees, eventually, despite her feelings against marrying young: "I wanted a *real* honeymoon with Edward. And, despite the danger he feared this would put me in, he'd agreed to try" (*Breaking Dawn* 22).

Ironically, all the traditional-gender-role-inverting negotiation is briefly rendered naught in a familiar scene wherein Edward becomes the seducer and Bella the resister. In the final pages of *Eclipse*, Edward decides that, since Bella seems to be doing everything to make everyone else happy, he should simply give her what they both want so desperately. By that point, though, she supports the idea of "doing this right," that is, withholding sex until they are married (619). In any case, Snitow's observation of 1970s mass-market romances is borne out in the Twilight quartet, which upholds the traditional sex-marriage economy: "sex means marriage and marriage, promised at the end, means, finally, there can be sex" (248).

The ephemeral, perpetually delayed nature of female sexuality as depicted in mass-market romances leads Snitow to note that the genre reinforces "the prevailing cultural code: pleasure for women is men. The ideal of romance presented in these books is a hungry monster that has gobbled up and digested all sorts of human pleasures" (253) except for "those that deal directly with arousing and satisfying men" (252). Despite the extended make-out scenes, in the Twilight quartet, sex means vaginal penetration by a penis, which leads one to wonder: if Bella's mother, Renée, had given Bella a vibrator for her fifteenth birthday, instead of Victoria's Secret lingerie (*Twilight* 298), could the quartet have been a trilogy? If either Edward or Bella understood sex to have a wider definition than just penetration, would Bella have been so insistent on doing "it" while she was human? Alas, these narrative options contravene the conventional construction of a mass-market romance heroine – who really cannot understand her own sexual potentials – and so are not available to Bella.

In vampire stories from Stoker's *Dracula* on, the act of sucking blood from a victim is the metaphorical equivalent to vaginal sex: intimate, invasive, often analogous to rape. Thus the delayed physical consummation of Bella and Edward's romance is not the entire point of the first three novels; that honour is shared with the consummation of Bella's desire to become a vampire, also perpetually imminent until well into the fourth book. Both sex and vampirization are anticipated using many of the same constructions. For example, the first time they make out, Edward tells Bella: "'Don't be afraid,'...his velvet voice unintentionally seductive" (*Twilight* 264). Later in the same volume he pretends to consider changing her: "'Right now?' he whispered, his breath blowing cool on my neck. I shivered involuntarily" (497). Though the latter quote refers to vampirization, and the former to sex, out of context, they are interchangeable. (For similar comparisons in the other volumes, see *New Moon* 495 and 518–19; *Eclipse* 187 and 274; and *Breaking Dawn* 85 and 373.) In the examples cited above, as well as those alluded to, Bella is the appropriately passive object of Edward's seduction, be it sexual or vampiric.

Thus, Snitow's analysis of the pornographic aspects of the1970s mass-market romance genre accurately describes the ways sex and its metaphorical equivalent, vampirization, are depicted in the Twilight quartet: both are intense, anticipatory, emotional and sadly limited, patterned as they are solely after the act that defines a heterosexual man's pleasure. Further, the books conflate sex and predation, the most significant marker of these books' Gothic character, as the third quarter of this essay will demonstrate. In the Twilight quartet, nothing – not shape-shifters, not vampires, not paranormal abilities – is more monstrous than Bella's psychological and physical submission to Edward.

Third Quarter: Pain

> Even as my lungs burned for more air and
> my legs cramped in the icy cold, I was content.
> I'd forgotten what real happiness felt like.
> Happiness. It made the whole dying thing pretty bearable.
>
> – Stephenie Meyer, *New Moon*

Pursuing Identity through Pain

The heroine of a mass-market romance will have the external skills that Snitow outlines – "passionate motherliness, good cooking, patience in adversity, efficient planning, and a good clothes sense" (249) – as well as the characteristics of blandness and mendacity (251). She will be unable to articulate her own desires adequately (258). But she will not necessarily be a masochist. In contrast, a Gothic heroine usually exhibits the traits of a romance heroine with one devastating addition; she will be driven to pursue pain and the men who can administer it, not only to prove that she is lovable, but also to provide her with a sense of identity.

According to Michelle A. Massé in *In the Name of Love*, masochism is "the end result of a long and varyingly successful cultural training" (3), which teaches girls to monitor themselves, to normalize the denial of active drives, to forget their pain and suffering as pain and suffering and to remember them as evidence of affection and their own lovability (3), precisely the amnesiac, masochistic path which Bella follows through the quartet.

Massé's literary analyses build upon the cultural criticism in Jessica Benjamin's *The Bonds of Love: Psychoanalysis, Feminism, and the Problem of Domination*, and so Massé explores literary depictions of masochism as formative of, and complicit in, the continued acceptance of masochism in contemporary culture. Thus, masochism lies "deep within identity, entangled with the need for love and recognition" (Massé 239). As a good romance heroine, Bella is alienated from understanding her own sexual desires; as a good Gothic heroine, she also fails to comprehend the sources of her pain: "the inhibition of active instincts that goes along with masochism limits a woman's ability to recognize her own suffering, to ask questions about it, and to act even when she gains such hard-won knowledge" (239).

Massé interprets Sigmund Freud's article "'A Child is Being Beaten': A Contribution to the Study of the Origin of Sexual Perversions" in a manner useful for explaining Bella Swan's unconscious penchant for pain: "Both the Gothic and psychoanalysis stage is what Freud calls the beating fantasy, in which a spectator watches someone being hurt by a dominant other" (3). Freud's essay describes his analysis of six sado-masochistic patients seen at different times in his career, and all of whom described to him independently a three-stage fantasy of being beaten. These stages, which did not vary significantly amongst the patients, are as follows: 1. My father is beating a child whom I hate; 2. (repressed) I am being beaten by my father, and 3. A child is being beaten (I am probably looking on) (185–86). Freud is explicit in determining that his readers realize the beating fantasy is precisely that – a fantasy. He notes that in his patients who had developed the beating fantasy "it might…be expected that the sight of another child being beaten at school would also be a source of similar enjoyment. But as a matter of fact this was never so" (180), an observation that would be reassuring in 1919 when he published "A Child is Being Beaten." Nonetheless, as discussed in the introduction to this book, subsequent cultural development led Jean Baudrillard to note that there's no longer any significant difference between reality and illusion (19), which obviates any comfort Freud's assurances may have once inspired.

Massé revises Freud's three stages in a manner which describes the situation of the Gothic heroine like Bella and her relationship to the authoritative hero like Edward, a revision which precisely describes the climactic events in *Twilight*:

1. "A bad man was hurting a woman." (Massé 74)
   Bella receives a phone call from the evil James, who puts Bella's mother, Renée, on the line; she is hysterical. James then threatens to torture Renée unless Bella comes to takes her place (*Twilight* 427–42).
2. "A bad man tried to hurt me." (Massé 74)
   Bella doesn't know until she's delivered herself to James that he has lured her with a recording of Renée's voice, stolen from her house in Phoenix. Although James then terrorizes and assaults Bella, breaking one of her legs, throwing her into a mirror, and finally biting her on the wrist, the deeper assault fails; he neither kills her nor turns her into a vampire.
3. "A good man saved me. Now we will live happily ever after." (Massé 74)
   Edward arrives in time to vanquish James and fulfill the first half of Massé's third part. The final clause is not fulfilled for two and a half more volumes when they work out the usual "happily ever after" of marriage.

Massé's revision of the beating fantasy describes the action at the end of *Twilight*, in microcosm, as well as the entire Twilight narrative, in macrocosm.

Stage One: Bella's Daddies

> My father is beating a child whom I hate.
>
> – Sigmund Freud, "A Child is Being Beaten"

> A bad man was hurting a woman.
>
> – Michelle A. Massé, *In the Name of Love*

In replacing "my father" with "a bad man," and "a child" with "a woman" Massé indicates that heroines trapped in the beating fantasy will be tremendously confused about their relationships with male progenitors. As Snitow predicts, "perhaps the heroes really are fathers – obscure, forbidding objects of desire" (250). Thus, it's not entirely *outré* that Bella has three daddies, two of whom should be beloveds, and one who shouldn't.

First, since Bella frames her relationship with her mother as that of parent to child – with Bella as parent (*Twilight* 4, 34, 106) – it's no great stretch that she also tends to replace her mother in the relationship with her father. She insists on calling him "Charlie"; that she cannot do so directly suggests it contravenes a taboo (*Twilight* 6, 59). By taking over the cooking at home, Bella relates to Charlie more as partner than child; for example, she leaves off her age-appropriate hanging out with Jacob and his friends in order to be home to prepare Charlie's supper (*New Moon* 140). Furthermore, at the cusp of her entrance into adulthood she moves from her childhood home with her mother to live with her father, an unattached adult man. Finally, when Edward deserts Bella and she's casting about for reasons to keep living, the only thing that keeps her going is the thought that "Charlie mattered, if nothing else did" (*New Moon* 75).

Since Bella behaves towards her father like a spouse, it is no great revelation to discover that she treats her beloveds like daddies. According to Freud, masochists formed by the beating fantasy "develop a special sensitiveness and irritability towards anyone whom they can include in the class of fathers" (195), which explains Bella's oddly vehement reactions toward Edward from the outset of their acquaintance: "I couldn't believe the rush of emotion pulsing through me – just because he'd happened to look at me for the first time in a half-dozen weeks. I couldn't allow him to have this level of influence over me. It was pathetic. More than pathetic, it was unhealthy" (*Twilight* 73–74). The first time Bella invites Edward into her father's house, she fantasizes about replacing Charlie with Edward – "I couldn't picture it, this godlike creature sitting in my father's shabby kitchen chair" (*Twilight* 292) – and when he does sit there "his beauty lit up the kitchen" (293). Even the music that Edward writes for Bella is a lullaby, rather than a love song (311). Thus Edward's character is couched in terms of a father figure to Bella.

Edward is also a menace specifically to her because her blood smells particularly tasty to him; Edward explains that there's "a name for someone who smells the way Bella does to me. They call her my *singer* – because her blood sings to me" (*New Moon* 490). Consequently, Bella is in constant danger of predation in his company. When he is least in control of himself, instead of focusing on self-control, Edward controls Bella. This makes her feel loved:

> His eyes were wild, his jaw clenched in acute restraint, yet he didn't lapse from his perfect articulation. He held my face just inches from his. He dazzled my eyes.
> "Should I...?" I tried to disengage myself, to give him some room.
> His hands refused to let me move so much as an inch. (*Twilight* 282–83; see also 302, 328, 345, 477–78)

As a result of that dangerous moment, Bella becomes "all the more besotted by him. It would cause me physical pain to be separated from him now" (283). Bella's enjoyment of Edward's authority over, and constraint of, her is evidence of her generically Gothic character:

> Like the Gothic heroine, so demurely exhibitionist and
> so dutifully subordinate before her all-powerful other,
> the masochist uses her passivity to seek recognition and
> to preserve a coherent identity as best she knows how.
> She follows the plot of heterosexual romance, the only
> plot in which culture allows her a leading role. Her very
> helplessness becomes the means through which she achieves
> acknowledgement, whether loving or punitive. (Massé 87–88)

Though both Charlie and Edward are father figures, it is Edward who is more authoritative, more dangerous and therefore preferred by the Gothic heroine, Bella.

The Quileute shape-shifter Jacob Black also takes on the attributes of a daddy to Bella, but never as effectively as Edward or Charlie. Jacob is a family friend of the Swans and the former owner of Bella's ancient truck. Although at sixteen, Jacob is younger than Bella (*Twilight* 146), they make a game of comparing their relative practical abilities which results in Jacob gaining years on her: "By the time we got back to La Push, I was twenty-three and he was thirty – he was definitely weighting skills in his favor" (*New Moon* 147, see also 206). Thus Bella rationalizes Jacob into an age nearly appropriate for a father, despite the fact that in some contexts – particularly in regard to her mother – Bella is inappropriately mature (*Twilight* 106). Furthermore, Jacob's process of development into a shape-shifter accelerates his maturation: "'We reach full growth inside of a few months when the werewolf gene gets triggered. It's one hell of a growth spurt.' He made a face. 'Physically, I'm probably twenty-five or something'" (*Eclipse* 120). Though Jacob's actual youth puts him at a disadvantage, his supernatural growth and game-awarded maturity ensure he is, if not on a par with

Edward and Charlie, at least in the running as a potential father figure.

Jacob's role in *Twilight* is small; he becomes much more important in *New Moon*, when he both discovers his shape-shifting ability and provides a refuge for Bella in the aftermath of Edward's abandonment. As a newly minted shape-shifter, Jacob is constantly at risk of turning into a wild predator: "'The hardest part is feeling...out of control,' he said slowly. 'Feeling like I can't be sure of myself – like maybe you *shouldn't* be around me, like maybe nobody should. Like I'm a monster who might hurt somebody'" (*New Moon* 345; see also 312, 348). Sweet, young, human Jacob's romantic pursuit of Bella makes her uncomfortable at the outset of *Twilight* (127), but when in *New Moon* he begins to mature into an unstable, supernatural creature with great potential to harm her, she treats him as a substitute for Edward (370–71).

Both Edward and Jacob love Bella; both restrain her – Edward physically and Jacob through the threat of provocation – and she is in dire danger whenever she is with either of them. Their similarities are so marked that in *New Moon* Bella dreams they are interchangeable:

Rain was falling and Jacob was walking soundlessly beside me, though beneath *my* feet the ground crunched like dry gravel. But he wasn't my Jacob; he was the new, bitter, graceful Jacob. The smooth suppleness of his walk reminded me of someone else, and, as I watched, his features started to change. The russet color of his skin leached away, leaving his face pale white like bone. His eyes turned gold, and then crimson, and then back to gold again. His shorn hair twisted in the breeze, turning bronze where the wind touched it. And his face became so beautiful that it shattered my heart. I reached for him, but he took a step away, raising his hands like a shield. And then Edward vanished. (276)

All three of Bella's daddy-beloveds (Charlie, Edward and Jacob) wield the implicit authority of age over her, whatever their calendar years, thereby fulfilling the romance convention that the hero must be older than the heroine (Snitow 251). However, only Edward constrains her when they are together, and causes her emotional pain when they are separated, which leads her to subject herself to physical pain. Thus, Edward is the most successful of Bella's daddies at being the "bad man [who] was hurting a woman" (Massé 74); she trusts only Edward to administer the pain that defines her.

Interlude: Another Alternative Daddy

It's feasible to consider Carlisle Cullen as an alternative daddy to Bella. As Edward's "maker," he is the patriarch of the vegetarian vampire clan, and he certainly fills the older-than-Bella stricture, as he was born in London in the 1650s (*Twilight* 335). Given Edward's reluctance to turn Bella, Carlisle is her second choice to infect her with vampire venom (*New Moon* 536), an act analogous to sex, and which would add several whiffs of incest to their relationship: sire as lover, father-in-law as lover, and, as the progenitor of both Bella and Edward, a promoter of sibling incest.

Stage Two, Part I: Violence Proves his Love

> (repressed) My father is beating me.
>
> – Sigmund Freud, "A Child is Being Beaten"

Freud's patients and the literary heroines that Massé discusses all act on the assumption that punishment from the father is an expression of his desire for her and is therefore to be sought: "The two conscious phases appear to be sadistic, whereas the middle and unconscious one is undoubtedly of a masochistic nature; its content consists in the child's being beaten by her father, and it carries with it the libidinal charge and the sense of guilt" (Freud

147

195–96). In the second stage, the subject is no longer an observer but participates as the beaten, which makes it "the most important and the most momentous [stage] of all. But we may say of it in a certain sense that it has never had a real existence" (Freud 185). It is both a libidinal pleasure and a source of guilt, the two elements necessary for the development of masochism according to Freud, who writes that the subject's statement "'My father loves me' was meant in a genital sense; owing to the regression it is turned into 'My father is beating me (I am being beaten by my father).' This being beaten is now a convergence of the sense of guilt and sexual love…. Here for the first time we have the essence of masochism" (Freud 189). A Gothic heroine's conflation of "guilt and sexual love" indicates her effort to develop an independent identity in a context that values her only as a receptacle of suffering.

Massé points out that Gothic heroines, like Matilda in the seminal eighteenth century Gothic novel *The Castle of Otranto* or O from the seminal twentieth century BDSM text *The Story of O*, "will forge a self through pain, and identify each fresh injury as a new token of affection" (104). Thus, "masochist" precisely describes Bella Swan who, by the third Twilight book, deeply self-identifies through the emotional pain she feels over hurting Edward and Jacob: "The sound of [Jacob's] agony still cut at me, somewhere deep in my chest. Right beside it was the other pain. Pain for feeling pain over Jacob. Pain for hurting Edward, too" (*Eclipse* 517). In "Breaking Faith: Disrupted Expectations and Ownership in Stephenie Meyer's Twilight Saga," Rachel Hendershot Parkin asserts that, since the Twilight books are of the romance genre, "the horizon of expectation included a belief in pain as the price for true love. Bella suffers excruciating pain after many of her choices in the first three novels. In particular, when Meyer sets Bella up for a choice between Edward and Jacob, she also sets Bella up for intense pain at the loss of whomever she does not choose" (75). Bella Swan has lost all sense of her pre-Forks identity and knows herself only through destructive and hurtful behaviours:

hers toward others, others' toward her and especially her guilt-ravaged behaviours toward herself.

Fortunately for Bella's masochism, violence is integral to both Edward and Jacob, held in check only by their often tenuous self-control, a situation which each recognizes in the other:

> *Edward to Bella*: "When I realized that you had put your life in the hands of werewolves, immature, volatile, the worst thing out there..." (*New Moon* 506)
>> *Jacob to himself/readers:* Maybe he'd smashed her like a bag of chips in his drive to get some? Because her life was less important to him than his own pleasure... (*Breaking Dawn* 149)

Edward indulges Bella's need for physical pain with alarming regularity: "He caught me up in his iron grip, crushing me to him. He seemed unaware of his watching family as he pulled my face to his, lifting my feet off the floor. For the shortest second, his lips were icy and hard against mine" (*Twilight* 403; see also *New Moon* 28, 451; *Eclipse* 539). So, too, does Jacob:

> I took his hand, and suddenly he yanked me – too roughly – right off the bed so that I thudded against his chest.
>
> "Just in case," he muttered against my hair, crushing me in a bear hug that about broke my ribs.
>
> "Can't – breathe!" I gasped. (*New Moon* 289–90; see also 222, 308; *Eclipse* 100, 507)

Bella counts their violence against her as proof of their love for her, because, as she observes, "One thing I truly knew – knew it in the pit of my stomach, in the center of my bones, knew it from the crown of my head to the soles of my feet, knew it deep in my empty chest – was how love gave someone the power to break you" (*New Moon* 219).

Sado-Scopophilic Interlude

Nowhere is Bella's masochism more clear than in her regard for Emily, the destined soulmate of Sam, the leader of the Quileute wolf pack. In an uncontrolled wolfie moment, Sam slashes Emily so that "the right side of her face was scarred from hairline to chin by three thick, red lines, livid in colour though they were long healed. One line pulled down the corner of her dark, almond-shaped right eye, another twisted the right side of her mouth into a permanent grimace" (*New Moon* 331). Bella sees those scars as emblems of Sam's adoration: "I watched him cross the room in one stride and take her face in his wide hands. He leaned down and kissed the dark scars on her right cheek before he kissed her lips" (333). She perceives them as beautiful: Emily "met my eyes, and I could suddenly see the symmetry underlying her deformity. Her face was still beautiful, and alive with a concern even more fierce than mine" (337). Bella wants to move from witness to participant in a love like that of Sam and Emily; Bella describes how in a dream "I stood in the forest again, but I didn't wander. I was holding Emily's scarred hand as we faced into the shadows and waited anxiously for our werewolves to come home" (341).

Stage Two, Part II: Pain Defines Her

> A bad man tried to hurt me.
>
> – Michelle A. Massé, *In the Name of Love*

In *Twilight*, monsters are not necessarily monstrous, which is the opposite of the situation in *Buffy the Vampire Slayer*, where the heroes have an inherent monstrosity to them. When Bella thinks that Jacob, Sam and the rest of the Quileute wolf pack have been killing hikers, she worries "it was bad enough that my best friend was a werewolf. Did he have to be a monster, too?" (*New Moon* 301). She is relieved to discover that they have been trying to protect the hikers, not kill them (308). Similarly, though she knows

Edward is a vampire with a constant thirst for human blood, she trusts not only that he will control that thirst, but also that he has a soul and is redeemed: "It seemed silly that this fact – the existence of his soul – had ever been in question, even if he was a vampire. He had the most beautiful soul, more beautiful than his brilliant mind or his incomparable face or his glorious body" (*Breaking Dawn* 24). Bella knows neither Jacob nor Edward is human but, in her estimation, it doesn't follow that they are monsters. Bella's overvaluation of Edward's human soul and of Jacob's humane heart prompts her to cherish their violence toward her as proof that she is worthy of their affection.

In this masochistic context, it makes sense that when Edward leaves Bella in *New Moon*, Bella loses her identity; for a masochist "to be ignored – not to merit any kind of attention, no matter what form it takes – is to disappear as a self," while "to be beaten is proof of existence and even of lovableness" (Massé 105). Thus, when Bella attends a horror movie with Jessica, she identifies with the zombies (*New Moon* 106). Despite Jacob's and Charlie's best efforts, Bella feels her life is without meaning when Edward is gone.

Bella feels eviscerated by Edward's absence: "It was a crippling thing, this sensation that a huge hole had been punched through my chest, excising my most vital organs and leaving ragged, unhealed gashes around the edges that continued to throb and bleed despite the passage of time" (*New Moon* 118; see also 123, 193, 219, 228, 233, 267). Without him to administer her pain, Bella not only feels emotional anguish; she pursues emotional and physical pain in order to hear what she knows is a delusion of his voice. She discovers this coping mechanism when she abandons her friend Jessica in order to approach some disreputable looking men hanging around outside a bar. She hears a voice say:

"Bella, stop this right now!"

My muscles locked into place, froze me where I stood. Because it wasn't Jessica's voice that rebuked me now. It was a furious voice, a familiar voice, a beautiful voice – soft like velvet even though it was irate.

It was *his* voice. (*New Moon* 111)

When she continues in the putatively dangerous situation and one of the men she's approaching greets her, the voice in her head emits "an exquisite snarl" (114). After that she courts danger, firstly by riding the motorcycle that puts her in the emergency room again and again:

"This is reckless and childless and idiotic, Bella," the velvet voice fumed. (184)

"Do you want to kill yourself, then? Is that what this is about?" the other voice spoke again, his tone severe. (186)
"No, Bella!" the angry, honey-sweet voice ordered in my ear. "Watch what you're doing!" (187)

My velvet-voiced delusion had yelled at me for almost five minutes. (193)

Secondly, by entering the monster-infested woods alone, where she encounters the hungry, unrepentant vampire, Laurent:

The voice responded with a low snarl. (238)

The frantic growling in my head made it hard to hear. (240)
"Threaten him," the beautiful delusion ordered, his voice distorted with dread. (241)

The sound of Edward's furious roar echoed distantly in the back of my head. (242)

Thirdly, by provoking Jacob before he's gained full control over his werewolf nature:

The warning words came in Edward's voice again. (268)
"Be very careful, Bella," his velvet voice warned. (307)

Fourthly, by discovering that Victoria wants to torture and kill her:

In my head, Edward snarled in fury at the name. (313)

Lastly, by diving off a cliff during a violent storm:

It was only when he was disapproving like this that I could hear the true memory of his voice… (358)
He was angry now, and the anger was so lovely (359)

and subsequently nearly drowning in the undertow:

"Fight!" he yelled. "Damn it, Bella, keep fighting." (360)

Edward is also hero-typically honourable and courteous, but no memory of those traits brings his voice to Bella in his absence. Nor does the Cullens' empty house evoke the delusion (161). It's only when she courts danger that Bella hears his

furious,
     beautiful,
irate,
snarling,
     soft,
fuming,
severe,
     velvet,
yelling,
growling,
     exquisite,

threatening,
roaring,
    lovely,
warning,
disapproving,
    honey-sweet,
angry,
damning

voice. She really would "do anything for that voice" (*New Moon* 307) because "even the pain she may inflict upon herself can be a way of maintaining control of her own identity and of warding off more dangerous external threats" (Massé 51). The risk to herself must be real to evoke the delusion, however, so the "anything" she "would do" must have the potential to cause her serious bodily harm and optimally result in a judicious soupçon of physical pain.

When Edward and Bella get back together at the end of *New Moon*, nothing that he says proves his love to her. Eventually, though, she is persuaded by her own memories of this delusional, verbal violence:

> "I could remember how your voice sounded when you were angry. I could hear it, like you were standing right there next to me. Mostly I tried not to think about you, but this didn't hurt so much – it was like you were protecting me again. Like you didn't want me to be hurt.
>
> "And, well, I wonder if the reason I could hear you so clearly was because, underneath it all, I always knew that you hadn't stopped loving me." (*New Moon* 526)

She has to hurt herself in order to evoke the delusion of a protector who is more dangerous to her than anything else, and this closed circuit proves his love for her? It makes sense only within the claustrophobic economy of the beating fantasy.

The Twilight novels present Gothic plots which "erase the process of the masochist's formation in order to consequently point insistently at the happy ending ideology promises" (Massé 3). The first three Twilight novels point insistently toward Bella's marriage to, and vampirization by, Edward. By focusing readers' attention on the potential for that "happy" ending, the books distract us from her consistently reinscribed masochism.

Snitow observes that in mass-market romances, "a brutal male sexuality is magically converted to romance" (353). In the Twilight books, the potential romance heroes don't just exhibit "cruelty, callousness, coldness, [and] menace" (248) in their characters; the metaphor has become actual – both are supernatural predators. Like a typical victim of relationship abuse, Bella is at physical risk every second she spends with either of her beloveds. Like a typical mass-market romance heroine, Bella accepts that physical and emotional pain and danger are inescapable aspects of love. And like a typically masochistic Gothic heroine, Bella learns to "find her pleasure in pain, satisfy active strivings through passivity, and know her subjectivity only through an other. She must come to find the malformation comfortable and insist that it is what she herself wanted" (Massé 77).

Auto-Erotic Interlude

A good novel tells us the truth about its hero;
but a bad novel tells us the truth about its author.

– G. K. Chesterton, *Heretics*

The Gothic heroine's "own body is cordoned off as a place to explore, as a child by others, and later by herself. The masturbation that so often marks the close of the beating fantasies Freud's virgin patients imagine may, like the role of spectator, remove her from the marriage economy and is to be avoided" (Massé 82). When Bella discovers that Edward watched her sleep for weeks, neither of them mentions her masturbating, just talking in her sleep. Ergo, it's safe to assume that she doesn't indulge in the auto-eroticism which would render her unmarriageable. Freud observes that "subjects [of the beating fantasy] without recourse to masturbation develop an elaborate superstructure of day-dreams [around] the masochistic beating-phantasy. The function of this superstructure was to make possible a feeling of satisfied excitation, even though the masturbatory act was abstained from" (190). Certainly, the Twilight novels constitute such an elaborate superstructure.

Stage Three: Becoming the Beater

> A child is being beaten.
>
> – Sigmund Freud, "A Child is Being Beaten"

> A good man saved me. Now we will live
> happily ever after.
>
> – Michelle A. Massé, *In the Name of Love*

In the third stage of Freud's iteration of the beating fantasy, all action, gender, person and libidinal content has been removed; the impulse to cause others to be beaten remains and indicates sadistic content. The subject fantasizes her genderless self, observing her father beating those whom she wants to hurt:

> The girl, who has even renounced her sex, and who has on the whole accomplished a more thorough going work of repression, nevertheless does not become freed from her father; she does not venture to do the beating herself; and since she has herself become a boy [in her fantasies], it is principally boys whom she causes to be beaten. (Freud 200)

In *Breaking Dawn*, the final book of the Twilight quartet, Bella cannot survive without becoming a vampire and therefore as diamond-hard as her beloved Edward; it is as if the statue turned Pygmalion to marble.

Even though she is virtually invulnerable after the transformation, Bella repeatedly dreams about the encroaching threat to a mysterious child she is sworn to protect, until the scene becomes real in the climactic confrontation: the threat is the decadent vampire aristocracy, headed by the Volturi; the mysterious child is her daughter, Renesmee. In each dream iteration of the scene, Bella's emotions move from fear and despair over the risk to the child, her life, and her vampire and human families – "*We're going to die*, I thought in panic" (*Breaking Dawn* 367; see also 118, 681) – to sadistic, aggressive rage – "And then, like a burst of light from a flash, the whole scene was different. Yet nothing changed – the Volturi still stalked toward us, poised to kill. All that really changed was how the picture looked to me. Suddenly, I was hungry for it. I wanted them to charge. The panic changed to bloodlust" (118–19; see also 367–68, 683). At the same time that she gains great strength by being changed from human to vampire, Bella's dreams change from the second stage's repressed, passive masochism to the third stage's active sadism. She wants to cause physical pain, not just experience it. Despite this desire, Bella remains true to the passivity of the Gothic heroine; she never develops sufficient agency to deliberately hurt anyone. As an exemplary heroine, she is limited to watching, protecting and being hurt.

Fourth Quarter: Complicity

Why would I fight when I was so happy where I was?
Even as my lungs burned for more air and
my legs cramped in the icy cold, I was content.
I'd forgotten what real happiness felt like.
Happiness. It made the whole dying thing pretty bearable.

– Stephenie Meyer, *New Moon*

Bella Transformed

The first quarter of this essay argues that the Twilight novels fit the 1970s mass-market romance formula, which led to the second quarter's assertion that they're also pornographic by examining the Twilight texts in the light of Snitow's point that women's pornography focuses on repetition rather than climax and so is fitted to the romance genre. The third quarter shows how the books are Gothic in that they normalize the heroine's need for pain, which serves as proof not just that she is loved, but that she is individuated; thus far the romance and Gothic elements of the heroine's character go together.

The third book in the quartet, *Eclipse*, ends with the protagonists' betrothal, thus completing the mass-market romance's usual narrative trajectory (Regis 14). *Breaking Dawn*, the fourth book, enters the bailiwick of the Marital Gothic, which Massé describes as beginning "with, or shortly after, marriage.... Perfect love supposedly has cast out fear, and perfect trust in another has led to the omission of anxiety" (20). Ideally, marriage is not just the cleaving together of a romantically inclined couple; if that were the case, Bella could have insisted on decamping to Las Vegas for her nuptials, as was her first impulse (*New Moon* 541). Instead, she is a passive participant in the full society-building exercise (her sister-in-law-to-be Alice

Cullen organizes the entire wedding) which draws together both families – unequally, as the human Swans don't realize the Cullens are vampires – and their extremely various communities, including readers, to witness and condone the match.

In the claustrophobically patriarchal tradition of the Marital Gothic, the father delivers the heroine to the husband who, like Pygmalion, "will remold her, forever hold her, and whose loving clasp will be like a gate closing off all exit" (21); Bella describes the core of her wedding ceremony as the moment when "Charlie took my hand and, in a symbol as old as the world, placed it in Edward's. I touched the cool miracle of his skin, and I was home" (*Breaking Dawn* 49). This prepares the way for the beginning of a Marital Gothic narrative in which "the husband who was originally defined by his opposition to the unjust father figure slowly merges with that figure" (Massé 20). Edward remoulds Bella more extremely than ever did a Harlequin hero his heroine but at least as much as Pygmalion did his statue: he makes her into a vampire like himself, a mortal danger to everyone she knew before their marriage. Unbeknownst to most of the wedding guests, this transformation is what they are asked to condone.

Prior to their marriage, Edward is controlling: he lets himself into Bella's room to watch her sleep (*Twilight* 293); he tries to keep her from friends he doesn't like (*Eclipse* 34); and when she disobeys him, she fears his response (132). Platt observes, "Meyer employs conservative social values like the policing of female desire, the protection of female virtue from ruin, the importance of marriage, and the sanctity of life as key plot devices, creating a world in which vulnerable women need to be protected at all times, both from external forces and from their own desires" (72–73). Readers accept this state of affairs because Bella narrates the story, with the exception of *Eclipse*'s epilogue and the middle section of *Breaking Dawn*. As the wielder of the all-powerful point of view, Bella presents Edward as the object of her subjective desire; so led, readers gloss over his menacing behaviours.

But the erosion of Bella's identity through pernicious, increasingly violent self-harm over the course of the quartet means that her subjectivity simply cannot hold. In the final book, Bella breaks down, necessitating an awkward shift in point of view; for a while she becomes the object of Jacob's subjective narrative. When the narration shifts again, ostensibly it returns to Bella, but this is Nouvelle Bella, now transformed into an angelic vampire, the perfected object of Edward's desire.

Breaking Dawn, Book I: Human Bella

At the beginning of *Breaking Dawn*, Bella is entrapped in the repressed second stage of the beating fantasy. The morning after their first night of sex, Bella wakes "too happy to change anything, no matter how small" (86). Edward, on the other hand, feels terrible because he battered her during their lovemaking. She peers at herself in the mirror to see what exactly has appalled him:

> I'd definitely had worse. There was a faint shadow across one
> of my cheekbones, and my lips were a little swollen, but other
> than that, my face was fine. The rest of me was decorated
> with patches of blue and purple. I concentrated on the
> bruises that would be the hardest to hide – my arms and my
> shoulders. They weren't so bad. My skin marked up easily. By
> the time a bruise showed I'd usually forgotten how I'd come
> by it. Of course, these were just developing. I'd look even
> worse tomorrow. (95–96)

Her bruises signify intimacy, with the difference from sex being that Bella can comment on them openly. In a classic instance of Freudian transference, she obsesses about the pillow feathers stuck in her hair instead of the bruises on her body. And she is appalled by Edward's subsequent declaration: "He paused, lifting his chin slightly. And then he spoke again with firm conviction. 'I will not make love with you until you've been changed. I will never hurt you again'" (98). This is the last thing she wants.

According to Camille Paglia, in a sado-masochistic relationship like that of Bella and Edward,

> his pleading reactivates the maternal in her. She forgives him. Never is he more open, vulnerable, and intimate than when he begs for a second chance – "I'll never do it again." His tenderness and affection enamor her. *She is addicted to the apology.* She is overwhelmed by sensory ecstasy, by the heightened passions of rage and frenzy yielding to the melting reunion of boy and mother, who nestles her son against her bosom. As in the self-flagellation of medieval Catholicism, physical pain may produce spiritual exaltation. The battered woman stays because she thinks she sees the truth and because secretly, she knows she is victorious. (44)

Despite Edward's resolve to abstain, Bella seduces him again (*Breaking Dawn* 110) and again (117), though never with the apologetic payoff of the first time. Her perverse delight in the pain she receives from her husband indicates that she has not matured beyond the beating fantasy's second stage. Bella's bruises signify that she remains a good Gothic heroine, in whom "the active drives must be channeled, expressed, and used in some fashion, for it is almost impossible to erase them entirely. They are therefore turned 'round upon the subject's own self' so that the self becomes its own object. Then another who can act out active urges with impunity is assigned the role of subject" (Massé 84; internal quote from Freud's "On Transformation of Instinct as Exemplified in Anal Eroticism" 126). Initially, the Pygmalion myth's application to the Twilight quartet seemed obvious: narrator Bella is the author of Edward, the animated statue who fulfills her dreams of the perfect boyfriend. That idea disintegrated with the understanding that Edward creates from bland Bella a perfect virtuous beauty whom he wants to marry. He does this by constraining her behaviour, by causing deep shifts in her desires (from wanting to attend college somewhere sunny to becoming a teen bride and mother), and eventually by siring her as a vampire. As the beloved, the one upon whom action is taken, Bella becomes the object of Edward's subjectivity; rather than the hero learning to become softer, the heroine must become hard.

In order for Bella to condone Edward's usurpation of her subject-identity, she must overvalue him, and undervalue herself: "the other to whom one yields one's own subjectivity has to be held worthy of such a gift. Given the gift's value, the other is necessarily overvalued. Furthermore, there must be a pay-off in pleasure, a grafting of sexuality onto the aggression of the overvalued other" (Massé 84). Bella has overvalued Edward from the beginning of their relationship, as she tells him in *Twilight*:

> "Well, look at me," I said, unnecessarily as he was already staring. "I'm absolutely ordinary – well, except for bad things like all the near-death experiences and being so clumsy that I'm almost disabled. And look at you." I waved my hand toward him and all his bewildering perfection. (*Twilight* 210; see also *New Moon* 65; *Eclipse* 233; *Breaking Dawn* 42)

Her contentment with the beating she receives on their first night of wedded bliss indicates that the graft of sexuality onto aggression has taken. It also indicates complicit acquiescence in her transformation from the quartet's subject narrator to the created object.

Breaking Dawn, Book II: Naught Bella

When Bella marries, she gives up her prior identity for that of Edward's annex, the hero who lets her prove her love by taking on all of the hurt he can cause her, including guilt over hurting her. But when she becomes pregnant, she finds an even richer source of pain to shore up her eroding sense of self, a trove more tightly bound to her than even her husband, which explains her abandonment of Edward and his plan for an abortion (*Breaking Dawn* 138). Edward is not prepared to be dumped, as Jacob observes when they return from their honeymoon: "I knew I would have to live a lot more, suffer a lot more, to ever understand the searing agony in Edward's eyes" (176).

Never has Bella had such a fecund source of hurt to buttress her masochistic identity. The fetus' vampire-human hybridity means that her merely human body cannot sustain the gestation: in just a few days, it starves her (235), requires her to ingest blood (249–50), breaks her ribs (274), and then her pelvis (321). The burden of the developing vampire-human fetus so consumes Bella that she can no longer carry the narrative. Jacob – now third-best-beloved, after the fetus and Edward – takes over. His point of view becomes that of the readers, trapped by a perverse fascination into witnessing Bella's surrender of every vestige of her pre-Edward identity: "even knowing that it was almost over, the hold she had on me only got harder to break" (*Breaking Dawn* 296). Massé describes the readers' complicity in the beating fantasy in a manner that explains our continued fascination with the Gothic Twilight narrative:

> As readers we too are spectators/accomplices to the Gothic's repetitive display of masochism. The insidious lure of audience participation parallels characters' regression from the spectator's analytic scrutiny of "a child being beaten" to center stage's heady, unself-conscious immersion in aggression and sexuality generated by the other serving as subject, beating because he loves. (192)

We look through Jacob's eyes, by turns identifying with Bella and her sacrificial dissolution, and then with Edward and his knowledge that his control has been rejected by his beloved so that he can no longer "help" her. Jacob so identifies with Edward that he follows the vampire's hopeless lead in attempting to persuade Bella to abort the vampire hybrid, in favour of having "puppies" with him (*Breaking Dawn* 185, 193); Edward so identifies with Jacob's despair after her subsequent, out-of-hand rejection that he gives Jacob the keys to his Aston Martin Vanquish in a fruitless, vicarious attempt to run from the problem of Bella's impending demise (330).

With the birth of Renesmee, readers and Jacob discover that the strength of his attraction to Bella was actually due to the fetus she carried. One of the more bizarre aspects of the wolf shape-shifters is involuntary imprinting; they are at the mercy of biology in terms of life partner, and any individual in the pack may suddenly find himself indelibly, irrevocably attracted to some stranger, for life. The wolf has no choice in the matter; the beloved does, but in Twilight, they are all so flattered by their wolf's abject devotion that they acquiesce. Jacob imprints on the newborn Renesmee.

Jacob's unconscious captivation by his own future beloved, masked by a romance of mythic proportion (that of Bella and Edward), is an apposite metaphor for readers' fascination with a romance that, unconsciously or otherwise, grudgingly or with eager anticipation, most of us hope to experience: "Although the Twilight series offers fans a range of romantic relationships with which to identify, Twilight directs readers' and viewers' attention to the most arguably traditional and unequal one in the series – the relationship between Edward Cullen and Bella Swan. Indeed, the Edward-Bella relationship was the most frequently desired by the adult and teen fans in our study" (Behm-Morawitz, Click and Aubrey 152).

Breaking Dawn, Book III: Nouvelle Bella

Three monumental things happen at the birth of Renesmee, the first being the birth itself. Bella has never been comfortable with receiving gifts from Edward: "But how could I let him give me things when I had nothing to reciprocate with? He, for some unfathomable reason, wanted to be with me. Anything he gave me on top of that just threw us more out of balance" (*New Moon* 13). Finally, though, Bella has something she can give Edward and his family that they cannot otherwise get. (In typically masochistic self-deprecation, she discounts her own choice to become part of their family.) In the Twilight universe, vampires' bodies are frozen in their state at the time they were turned, and so the females can never become pregnant, though the males remain virile. Furthermore, turning children into vampires is taboo, because of the baby vampires' perpetual lack of control (*Breaking Dawn* 547). Despite this, all Edward's sister Rosalie wants is "to marry someone who love[s] *me*, and have pretty babies" (*Eclipse* 162). The maternal Esme was available to be turned into a vampire because, as she relates, my "'first and only baby…died just a few days after he was born, the poor tiny thing,' she sighed. 'It broke my heart – that's why I jumped off the cliff'" (*Twilight* 368). Thus, in bearing Edward's child, Bella finds a way to satisfy her own need for pain, and simultaneously "give back" to Edward and the rest of her vampire family.

The second momentous change that occurs with Renesmee's birth is the controversial imprinting of Jacob on the newborn, which explains why the pregnant Bella was always so happy to see Jacob: the fetus within her was calling to its soulmate. Despite the studied introduction of Jacob's imprinting into the Twilight novels – preparing it with several earlier examples of imprinting, including that between two-year-old Claire and adolescent Quil (*Breaking Dawn* 151–55); the comic treatment of Bella and Edward's outrage (448–51); Bella's slow realization that if she and Edward die, she can entrust Jacob with their daughter (645, 723); the introduction of another human-vampire hybrid, Nahuel, as a potential rival to Jacob (748) – and the repeated declaration that "it's not like that" (450, 750; "that" being a sexual attraction), it is *exactly* that. At best,

165

Jacob's imprinting on Renesmee condones arranged marriage and child betrothal.

Bearing Edward's child is the transaction that ushers Bella into the Cullen family completely; since her human body cannot survive the labour, the only way she can be saved is by what Jacob calls "emergency vampirization" (*Breaking Dawn* 191). Thus, the third momentous occurrence at Renesmee's birth is Bella's rebirth, through monumental agony, as a vampire. She describes the pain of her final stage of changing over:

> The whole of my existence did not outweigh this pain. Wasn't worth living through it for one more heartbeat.
>
> Let me die, let me die, let me die.
>
> And, for a never-ending space, that was all there was. Just the fiery torture, and my soundless shrieks, pleading for death to come. Nothing else, not even time. So that made it infinite, with no beginning and no end. One infinite moment of pain. (*Breaking Dawn* 377–78, see also 374–86)

In the midst of changing, Bella searches for the strength to suffer the change silently and save Edward concurrent pangs of guilt. First she looks for inspiration within her own identity, then in the identities of the people she loves:

> I held the blackness of nonexistence at bay by inches.
>
> It wasn't enough, though – that determination. As the time ground on and on and the darkness gained by tiny eighths and sixteenths of my inches, I needed something more to draw strength from.
>
> I couldn't pull even Edward's face into view. Not Jacob's, not Alice's or Rosalie's or Charlie's or Renée's or Carlisle's or Esme's... Nothing. It terrified me, and I wondered if it was too late....
>
> Renesmee. (374–75)

The thought of her child is the spar to which Bella clings in her days of burning change, and which keeps her quiet during her transformation. (Her silence leads Carlisle and Edward to believe that morphine blunted her agony. She determines never to let Edward know that, in a truly masochistic payoff, the drug kept her mute even though she felt every excruciating moment [*Breaking Dawn* 397].) Bella has found a new identity – mother – which moves her to the third stage of the beating fantasy.

Maternity transforms Bella into someone indefatigable and absolutely gorgeous. When first she looks into a mirror after being vamped, she describes what she sees:

> My first reaction was an unthinking pleasure. The alien
> creature in the glass was indisputably beautiful, every bit as
> beautiful as Alice or Esme. She was fluid even in stillness, and
> her flawless face was pale as the moon against the frame of
> her dark, heavy hair. Her limbs were smooth and strong, skin
> glistening subtly, luminous as a pearl.
>
> My second reaction was horror.
>
> Who was she? At first glance, I couldn't find my face
> anywhere in the smooth, perfect planes of her features.
> (*Breaking Dawn* 403)

Bland, accident-prone Bella no longer exists; she has been reborn without flaw. Speaking of the "Christian fundamentalist model of the twice-born," Adrienne Rich observes:

> The desire to be twice-born is, I believe, in part a longing
> to escape the burdens, complications, and contradictions
> of continuity…. In the desire to be twice-born there is a
> good deal of self-hatred. Too much of ourselves must be
> deleted when we erase our personal histories and abruptly
> dissociate ourselves from who we have been. We become less
> dimensional than we really are. The dialectic between change

and continuity is a painful but deeply instructive one, on
personal life as in the life of a people. (143; see also Hawes)

Nouvelle Bella is so much more beautiful, more graceful and stronger
than her human self that she, Jacob and the reader question whether
she is the same person. She's the ugly duckling who was Cullen-ed,
and so never completed her full fledging as Bella Swan.

One thing that Bella's vampiric renovation failed to change was
her sense of relative worthlessness in comparison with Edward.
The first word out of her changed mouth is "Oops" (*Breaking Dawn*
393), an allusion to her first kiss with Edward. In that instance, the
blood rushing to her cheeks nearly caused him to kill her (*Twilight*
282); now she's in danger of hurting him, because new vampires'
bodies are so suffused with the blood of their human life they are
preternaturally strong even for vampires. "Oops" is significant for
more than the internal reference. It is barely a word, a peeping
sound that admits error and asks forgiveness, and Bella utters it
when she has never been stronger or more magnificent.

Bella-as-mother graduates to the third, sadistic stage of Freud's
beating fantasy: "A child is being beaten." This change initially
appears in her prescient dreams of confrontation with the Volturi,
and later in the actual event. Her desire to cause pain is appropriately
maternal-protective, part of the Marital Gothic lexicon. Furthermore,
she never acts on her desire to beat the Volturi, because her special
vampiric talent is passive and defensive, as is appropriate for a Gothic
heroine. Bella is a Shield. Just as her placenta resisted all attempts
to look into it (*Breaking Dawn* 192), so Bella can hide her thoughts
from other vampires' paranormal talents, an extension of her human
thoughts' opacity to Edward's telepathy.

By the end of *Breaking Dawn*, Bella has learned to extend
her shield to protect not only her own mind but also those of
her vampire family and their allies (690), indicating how deeply
she has integrated maternal caretaking into her identity. When
psychically attacked by the Volturi, Bella finds her shield to be

"just as impenetrable as before. I flexed it now into a low, wide dome that arced over our company" (702), like a giant diaphragm. Not until the denouement of the final book does she master the skill of peeling back that shield enough to let someone in; that someone is, of course, her husband, Edward (752–53).

Because of Bella's shielding capability, she and her allies triumph by avoiding battle with the Volturi, which is a strong statement for conflict avoidance, though it makes for a weak climactic scene to the Twilight quartet. (Clarke disagrees with my evaluation of the climax as weak; she states, "Meyer also resists ending her series in an epic battle in the manner of Homer, Tolkien, Lewis, Rowling and countless other writers of fantasy. Instead of bloodshed, mental acuity of various sorts allows the newly extended Cullen–Wolf Pack clan to walk away the victors" ["Introduction" 6].) Thus, even though Bella briefly embodies the third, sadistic stage of the beating fantasy, her subsequent joyous submission to her husband suggests that she's still more comfortable in the unconscious, masochistic second stage. Never having recognized her own masochism, she has done nothing to escape the repetitive trauma of the beating fantasy despite having become the most powerful vampire in existence. What makes her powerful is her capacity to absorb pain meant not just for her but for others as well.

"Happily Ever After"

When *Breaking Dawn* was published, the Twilight blogosphere burst with expressions of outrage (Hendershot Parkin 72). Fans were upset not because of the overt evidence of Bella's masochism, but because she becomes sexually active, actually and metaphorically. She is impregnated first with Edward's semen which gets her "with child," and subsequently with his venom which turns her into a vampire. To those who identified with Bella as a non-threat at the bottom of the food chain, her transformation into a top predator must have seemed *outré*, even though this change had been anticipated almost since the outset of the quartet (*Twilight* 383). Bella's pregnancy is necessary to solve the difficult narrative problem of finding a way for a virtuous woman to turn into a vampire without committing the sin of suicide. For a Gothic heroine who finds self-definition in self-destruction, suicide can be devilishly tricky to avoid. Bearing a child at the cost of her life doesn't just steer Bella clear of that particular moral morass; it elevates her to a state of near-grace before which her family's enemies learn to tremble.

Massé observes that it is not enough for a Gothic tale to obsessively repeat "the masochism in which its protagonists are so well trained" (239); it must also recruit. Massé's observation about the Marquis de Sade's eponymous heroine Justine is also true of Bella: "she, like…all masochists who internalize the strictures that bind them, replicates her condition" (Masse 139 note 15). On the face of it, this tenet doesn't seem to operate in the Twilight quartet. Neither Jessica nor Angela, Bella's best girlfriends in the high school, nor any of their lunch-room crowd follows her down the road to self-destructive behaviours. But, since "the Gothic genre is 'about' suffering women whose painful initiations provides some vague pleasure for women authors, characters, and *readers*" (Massé 1, italics added), the overwhelming popularity of the Twilight quartet, particularly among young women, indicates that Bella is very successful at recruiting amongst her readership. After all, as Charles Maturin writes in *Melmoth the Wanderer*, "the drama of terror has the irresistible power of converting its audience into its victims" (178).

Speaking not of fictional characters but of actual women, Massé points out that masochists are likely to "repeat [their] own experiences time and again – in life, in fantasy, and in the Gothic novel" (51), and also to "do to others what has been done to them and thus confirm their own agency and relative power" (51). The Twilight novels promote to their impressionable readership the unexamined assumption that romance is masochistic and "there never was any pain or renunciation, that the suffering [masochistic women] experience is really the love and recognition for which they long" (Massé 3–4). Such promotion, both in lived life and in fictional representations, has made masochism "a key issue in feminine identity" (2), because "the construction of the female fantasy...normalizes passivity and masochism" (68). Bella Swan provides a prime example of masochism's normalization. Through acceptance of her husband's violence and her unplanned pregnancy, she is apotheosized from bland, submissive victim into a triumphant, dominant aggressor (albeit passive-aggressor) who epitomizes fantasies of perpetual youth, conspicuous consumption and unprecedented wealth.

Masochism's normativity is further proven by the Twilight quartet's popularity: the series' translation rights were sold in nearly fifty countries; eighty-five million copies have been sold worldwide (Eulberg); Meyer was listed by MSN as one of the twelve most influential women in the US in 2008; and she was the first author ever to have penned all the books which occupied the top four slots in *USA Today*'s year-end bestseller list, also in 2008.

The Twilight quartet remains maniacally popular despite its reprehensible gender and social implications because of the clever insinuation of dark Gothic psychology in a light mass-market romance. Bella and Edward exhibit all the traits that Snitow attributes to the heroine and hero of a mass-market romance, including those which promote a pornography expressly designed for women. Concurrently, Bella is inherently Gothic in that she does not just accept the dissolution of her identity – she embraces it. I've previously discussed how Twilight revises the Pygmalion myth, in that Edward embodies the roles of both statue – Twilight's vampires are made of stone – and sculptor – in the ways he constrains Bella until she transforms from tabula rasa to perfect mate. But Bella too embodies both Pygmalion roles, with one significant difference: since Edward is already perfect in her eyes, it is she who must be carved into faultless virtue. Thus, over the course of the quartet, Bella consumes her own subjectivity to become the perfected object of Edward's affection.

Meyer's assertions, chronicled in Hendershot Parkin, that "Bella is not anti-feminist because of her choices, but rather an empowered heroine in that she does make choices, ones that allow her to draw strength from Edward" (68) are both false and naïve. Far from being free, Bella's choices follow the imperative of the beating fantasy within which she firmly remains at the close of the quartet. Though fans and anti-fans alike often express unease over Edward's stalking behaviours and Jacob's imprinting on the newborn Renesmee, I've never heard complaints about Bella's masochism, which to my mind makes her perversion the most dangerous of the three because it is the most insidiously normative. Research undertaken by Behm-Morawitz, Click and Aubrey shows that readers want a relationship like that of Edward and Bella more than any of the others depicted in the novel (152), which bears out Hendershot Parkin's observation of Meyer, who "makes her opinion of Bella and Edward's relationship clear – it is a healthy and natural one, if a bit unusual, and is based on Meyer's understanding and interpretation of the nature of true love" (Hendershot Parkin 68). Thus, as Rebecca Housel states "painted with the romantic, fictitious flourish of author Stephanie Meyer's pen, what in reality would be a horrific account of violence against women, all too familiar in today's media, becomes a dangerously romanticized fantasy for a primarily young female audience" (178). The popularity of the quartet indicates that a sado-masochistic construction of "true love" is widely accepted, and that nothing consumes consumers like a romance permeated by the Gothic. The Twilight books don't slake so much as stimulate readers' socially induced identification with a heroine who measures love by how much it hurts.

Acknowledgements

I'm daunted by the prospect of trying to remember all the people who helped me develop my writing skills over the past thirteen years – members of workshops in Halifax and in Fredericton; all those librarians who taught me successive generations of research methods, from card catalogues to internet-based databases; the students from my honours seminar on the Popular Gothic in 2005–06. Specific individuals who spring to mind for their help with the essays include Steven Bruhm and Peter Schwenger for early encouragement in exploring theories of the Gothic, and to Ronald Tetreault, Judith Thompson and Anthony Harding for inspiring me to research widely. Thanks are owed to my fellow writing residents at Hawthornden Castle in 2008 – Merle Bachman, Petra White, Moy McCrory, Tiffany Antone and Leszek Engelking – for their cheerful camaraderie. Thanks to Don McKay and Dionne Brand for their editorial work on parts of this manuscript at the Banff Writing Studio in 2009, and to my colleagues at St. Thomas University – Alan Bourassa, Christine Cornell, Elizabeth McKim and Andrea Schutz – for their ongoing encouragement in getting the manuscript off of my desk and out the door. Thanks also to Sandra Barry and the Board of The Elizabeth Bishop House for the space and time to work on the manuscript, and especially to Wolsak and Wynn publisher Noelle Allen for helping to shape this manuscript, her able assistant Ashley Hisson who is familiar with every word on every page, and Beth McAuley at The Editing

Company, Toronto, for reminding me that just because something was popular doesn't mean people remember it. Also, thank you to Lindsay Hodder for compiling the index.

Travel to and from the places mentioned above was expedited by the support of an SSHRC Research-Creation grant which also provided funds for release from teaching duties, and for hiring some of the most excellent research assistants I've ever had the pleasure to work with: Tina Northrop, Joel Rodgers, Andrew Titus, Jessica Boland, Shakti Brazier-Tompkins, Caroline Nadeau, Allyson Groves, Lisa Banks and Patrick O'Reilly.

Thanks always to Sharolyn Lee, Catherine Jenkins and Martha Young for decades-long friendships and hospitality. And thanks especially always already to Stephen Nelles.

Notes

An earlier version of "Chaos at the Mouth of Hell: *Buffy the Vampire Slayer* and the Columbine High School Massacre" was published as "Chaos at the Mouth of Hell: Why Columbine High School Massacre had Repercussions for *Buffy the Vampire Slayer*" in *Gothic Studies* 2, no. 1 (April 2000): 119–25.

An earlier version of "*Dark Angel*: A Recombinant Pygmalion for the 21st Century" was published in *Gothic Studies* 4, no. 2 (2002): 178–191.

An earlier version of "Creating People for Popular Consumption: Echoes of Pygmalion and 'The Rape of the Lock' in *A.I. Artificial Intelligence*" was published in *The Journal of Popular Culture* 40, no. 4 (August 2007): 683–699.

A version of "Flex and Stretch: The Inevitable Feminist Treatise on *Catwoman*" was published in *The Dalhousie Review* 91, no. 2 (Summer 2011): 151–67; excerpts of an earlier version appeared in *FemSpec* 7, no. 1 (2007).

SOURCES

Adorno, Theodor W., and Max Horkheimer. *Dialectic of Enlightenment*. Translated by John Cumming. London: Verso Classics, 1997.

A.I.: Artificial Intelligence. Directed by Steven Spielberg (Stanley Kubrick). Universal City, CA: DreamWorks Home Entertainment, 2002. DVD.

Aldiss, Brian. "Supertoys Last All Summer Long." Wired.com 5, no. 1 (January 1997). http://www.wired.com/wired/archive/5.01/ffsupertoys_pr.html.

Anderson, William S. "Notes to Book 7." In Ovid's *Metamorphoses*, Books 6–10, edited by William S. Anderson. Norman: University of Oklahoma Press, 1972.

Aubrey, Jennifer Stevens, Scott Walus, and Melissa A. Click. "Twilight and the Production of the 21st Century Teen Idol." In Click, Aubrey and Behm-Morawitz, *Bitten by Twilight*, 225–41.

Bane, Kelsey. "Starting Over." *Teen People*, August 1999.

Batman Returns. Directed by Tim Burton. Burbank, CA: Warner Home Video, 2002. DVD.

"*Batman Returns* (1992)." Internet Movie Database. Accessed July 17, 2005. http://www.imdb.com/title/tt0103776/.

"*Batman* (1966)." Internet Movie Database. Accessed July 17, 2005. http://www.imdb.com/title/tt0060153/.

Baudrillard, Jean. *Simulacra and Simulation*. Translated by Sheila Faria Glaser. Ann Arbor: University of Michigan Press, 2003.

Behm-Morawitz, Elizabeth, Melissa A. Click, and Jennifer Stevens Aubrey. "Relating to Twilight: Fans' Responses to Love and Romance in the Vampire Franchise." In Click, Aubrey and Behm-Morawitz, *Bitten by Twilight*, 137–54.

Benjamin, Jessica. *The Bonds of Love: Psychoanalysis, Feminism, and the Problem of Domination*. New York: Pantheon, 1988.

Bergman, Benjamin. "Tragedy in Taber." *Maclean's*, May 10, 1999.

Bloustien, Geraldine. "Fans with a lot at stake: Serious play and mimetic excess in *Buffy the Vampire Slayer*." *European Journal of Cultural Studies* 5, no. 4 (November 2002): 427–50.

Botting, Fred. *Gothic*. New York: Routledge, 1996.

Brave. Directed by Mark Andrews, Brenda Chapman and Steve Purcell. Burbank, CA: Walt Disney Studios Motion Pictures, 2012. Theatrical Release.

Brown, Bill. "How to Do Things with Things (A Toy Story)." *Critical Inquiry* 24, no. 4 (Summer 1998): 935–64.

Buffy the Vampire Slayer. Created and produced by Joss Whedon. Los Angeles: 20th Century Fox Home Entertainment, 2002–04. DVD.

Burnett, Tamy. "'Just A Girl': The Community-Centered Cult Television Heroine, 1995–2007." PhD diss., University of Nebraska, 2010. ETD collection for University of Nebraska – Lincoln (AAI3398389). http://digitalcommons.unl.edu/dissertations/AAI3398389.

Burroughs, D.B. "Comments on *Catwoman*." Internet Movie Database. Accessed July 17, 2005. http://us.imdb.com/title/tt0327554/#comment (comment now deleted).

Bütz, Michael R. "The Vampire as a Metaphor for Working with Childhood Abuse." *The American Journal of Orthopsychiatry* 63, no. 3 (July 1993): 426–31.

Byrne, Bridget. "Banned 'Buffy' on the Internet." *E!Online*, June 3, 1999. Accessed June 3, 1999. http://ca.eonline.com/news/38258/banned-buffy-on-the-internet.

Cameron, James. "Cameron Unveils Dark Angel." MrShowBiz.com. July 23, 2000.

"*Cat Girl* (1957)." Directed by Alfred Shaughnessy. Internet Movie Database. Accessed July 17, 2005. http://www.imdb.com/title/tt0050235/.

"*Cat People* (1942)." Directed by Jacques Tourneur. Internet Movie Database. Accessed July 17, 2005. http://www.imdb.com/title/tt0034587/.

"*Cat People* (1982)." Directed by Paul Schrader. Internet Movie Database. Accessed July 17, 2005. http://www.imdb.com/title/tt0083722/.

Catwoman. Directed by Pitof. Burbank, CA: Warner Home Video, 2005. DVD.

"Catwoman (2004)." Internet Movie Database. Accessed July 17, 2004. http://www.imdb.com/title/tt0327554/.

Chisholm, Patricia. "Teens Under Siege." *Maclean's*, May 3, 1999.

Clarke, Amy M. "Introduction: Approaching Twilight" In Clarke and Osborn, *The Twilight Mystique*, 3–14.

Clarke, Amy M., and Marijane Osborn, eds. *The Twilight Mystique: Critical Essays on the Novels and Films*. Jefferson, NC: McFarland, 2010.

Clasen, Tricia. "Taking a Bite Out of Love: The Myth of Romantic Love in the Twilight Series." In Click, Aubrey and Behm-Morawitz, *Bitten by Twilight*, 119–34.

Click, Melissa A., Jennifer Stevens Aubrey and Elizabeth Behm-Morawitz, eds. *Bitten by Twilight: Youth Culture, Media, and the Vampire Franchise*. New York: Peter Lang, 2010.

Cohen, Jeffrey Jerome. "Monster Culture (Seven Theses)." In *Monster Theory: Reading Culture*, 3–25. Minneapolis: University of Minnesota Press, 1996.

Collins, Suzanne. *The Hunger Games*. New York: Scholastic, 2009.

Collins, Victoria E., and Dianne C. Carmody. "Deadly Love: Images of Dating and Violence in the 'Twilight Saga.'" *Affilia: Journal of Women and Social Work* 26, no. 4 (November 24, 2011): 382–94. doi:10.1177/0886109911428425.

Corliss, Richard. "Bang, You're Dead." *TIME*, May 3, 1999.

Cover, Rob. "From Butler to Buffy: Notes Towards a Strategy for Identity Analysis in Contemporary Television Narrative." *Reconstruction: Studies in Contemporary Culture* 4, no. 2 (Spring 2004). reconstruction.eserver.org/042/cover.htm.

Craigo-Snell, Shannon. "What Would Buffy Do? Feminist ethics and epistemic violence." *Jump Cut: A Review of Contemporary Media* 48 (Winter 2006).

Cullen, Dave. *Columbine*. New York: Hachette Digital, 2009.

Curran, Stuart. "Women readers, women writers." In *The Cambridge Companion to British Romanticism*, edited by Stuart Curran, 177–95. Cambridge: Cambridge University Press, 1993.

"*The Curse of the Cat People* (1944)." Directed by Robert Wise and Gunther von Fritsch. Internet Movie Database. Accessed July 17, 2005. http://www.imdb.com/title/tt0036733/.

Dark Angel. Created and produced by James Cameron and Charles H. Eglee. Los Angeles: 20th Century Fox Television, 2003–04. DVD.

Dark Knight Rises. Directed by Christopher Nolan. Burbank, CA: Warner Bros. Entertainment, 2012. Theatrical release.

Day, William Patrick. *In the Circles of Fear and Desire: A Study of Gothic Fantasy*. Chicago: University of Chicago Press, 1985.

DeLamotte, Eugenia C. *Perils of the Night: A Feminist Study of Nineteenth-Century Gothic*. Oxford: Oxford University Press, 1990.

Dick, Philip K. *Do Androids Dream of Electric Sheep?* New York: Ballantine, 1996.

Die Another Day. Directed by Lee Tamahori. Beverly Hills, CA: MGM Home Entertainment, 2003. DVD.

"Don't Blame TV, says Buffy Vampire." *Halifax Chronicle Herald*, July 27, 1999.

Dunn, Jancee. "Love at First Bite." *Rolling Stone*, April 2, 1998.

Early, Frances H., and Kathleen Kennedy, eds. *Athena's Daughters: Television's New Women Warriors*. Syracuse, NY: Syracuse University Press, 2003.

Early, Frances. "The Female Just Warrior Reimagined: From Boudicca to Buffy." In Early and Kennedy, *Athena's Daughters*, 55–65.

Edgeworth, Maria. *Belinda*. London: Macmillan, 1896. First published 1801.

Eglee, Charles H. "Freak Nation" Commentary. *Dark Angel*, season 2, episode 2. DVD. Created and produced by James Cameron and Charles H. Eglee. Los Angeles: 20th Century Fox Television, 2003.

Elektra. Directed by Rob Bowman. Los Angeles: Twentieth Century Fox, 2005. Web.

Elliott, Tara. "'Buffy vs. Dracula''s Use of Count Famous." *Journal of Dracula Studies* 8 (2006).

Emmanuel, Greg. Review of *Dark Angel*, created and produced by James Cameron and Charles H. Eglee. *Time Out New York*, September 7–14, 2000. Quoted in Dark Angel Media Quotes. 2000. http://www.darkangeltheseries. com/theseries/mediaquotes.htm (site discontinued).

Eulberg, Elizabeth. "Yen Press Announces *Twilight: The Graphic Novel, Vol. 1* Will Go On-Sale On March 16, 2010." Press Release, Hachette, New York, January 20, 2010.

Foucault, Michel. *The History of Sexuality*. Vol. 1, An Introduction. 1978. Translated by Robert Hurley. New York: Vintage Books, 1980.

Freud, Sigmund. "'A Child is Being Beaten': A Contribution to the Study of the Origin of Sexual Perversions (1919)." In *The Standard Edition of the Complete Psychological Works of Sigmund Freud*. Vol. 17, *An Infantile Neurosis and Other Works*, translated by James Strachey, 175–204. London: Hogarth Press, 1991.

———. "On Transformations of Instinct as Exemplified in Anal Eroticism (1917)." In *The Standard Edition of the Complete Psychological Works of Sigmund Freud*. Vol. 17, *An Infantile Neurosis and Other Works*, translated by James Strachey, 124–133. London: Hogarth Press, 1991.

———. "The Uncanny." In *The Collected Papers*. Vol. 4, 368–407. Translated by Joan Riviere. London: Hogarth Press, 1925.

Frøyland, Jan. *Introduction to Chaos and Coherence*. New York: Institute of Physics Publishing, 1992.

Geddes, John. "Is Gun Control the Solution?" *Maclean's*, May 3, 1999.

Gellar, Sarah Michelle. "Statement on the Season Finale of Buffy the Vampire Slayer." *Buffy the Vampire Slayer* Articles. May 1999. Accessed June 17, 1999. http://www.angelfire.com/ca4/bitethis/articles.html.

"Getting Past the Fear." *Teen People*, August 1999.

Gibbs, Nancy. "Special Report: The Littleton Massacre." *TIME*, May 3, 1999.

Gilbert, W. S. *Pygmalion and Galatea: An Entirely Original Mythological Comedy.* New York: T. H. French, 1912.

Gleick, James. *Chaos: Making a New Science.* New York: Viking, 1987.

Golden, Christopher, and Nancy Holder. *Buffy the Vampire Slayer: The Watcher's Guide.* New York: Pocket Books, 1998.

Goodson, A. C. "Frankenstein in the age of Prozac." *Literature and Medicine* 15, no. 1 (Spring 1996): 16–32. doi:10.1353/lm.1996.0004

Gottlieb, Richard M. "The Legend of the European Vampire: Object Loss and Corporeal Preservation." *Psychoanalytic Study of the Child* 49 (1994): 465–80.

Hand, Elizabeth. *Catwoman.* Novelization of the 2004 *Catwoman* movie. New York: Del Rey, 2004.

Harding, Anthony John. *The Reception of Myth in English Romanticism.* Columbia: University of Missouri Press, 1995.

Hawes, Janice. "Sleeping Beauty and the Idealized Undead: Avoiding Adolescence." In Clarke and Osborn, *The Twilight Mystique*, 163–78.

Hayles, N. Katherine. *Chaos Bound: Orderly Disorder in Contemporary Literature and Science.* Ithaca, NY: Cornell University Press, 1990.

Hendershot Parkin, Rachel. "Breaking Faith: Disrupted Expectations and Ownership in Stephenie Meyer's Twilight Saga." Jeunesse: *Young People, Texts, Cultures* 2, no. 2 (2010): 61–85.

Hendershot, Cyndy. *The Animal Within: Masculinity and the Gothic.* Ann Arbor: University of Michigan Press, 1998.

Hoberman, J. "The Dreamlife of Androids." *Sight and Sound* 11, no.9 (September 2001): 16–18.

Hoeveler, Diane Long. *Gothic Feminism: The Professionalization of Gender from Charlotte Smith to the Brontës.* University Park: Pennsylvania State University Press, 1998.

Holder, Nancy. "Lie to Me." In *The Angel Chronicles.* Vol. 1, 145–201. Based on the screenplay by Joss Whedon. New York: Pocket Books, 1998.

Housel, Rebecca. "The 'Real' Danger: Fact vs. Fiction for the Girl Audience." In Housel and Wisnewski, *Twilight and Philosophy*, 177–90.

Housel, Rebecca, and J. Jeremy Wisnewski, eds. *Twilight and Philosophy: Vampires, Vegetarians, and the Pursuit of Immortality.* Hoboken, NJ: John Wiley & Sons, 2009.

James, E. L. *Fifty Shades Darker.* New York: Vintage, 2012.

——. *Fifty Shades Freed.* New York: Vintage, 2012.

——. *Fifty Shades of Grey*. New York: Vintage, 2012.

Jeffers, Susan. "Bella and the Choice Made in Eden." In Clarke and Osborn, *The Twilight Mystique*, 137–51.

Jensen, Kristian. "Noble Werewolves or Native Shape-Shifters?" In Clarke and Osborn, *The Twilight Mystique*, 92–106.

Jones, Adam. "Case Study: The Montreal Massacre." Gendercide Watch. Accessed July 2010. http://www.gendercide.org/case_montreal.html.

Jowett, Lorna. "To the Max: Embodying Intersections in *Dark Angel*." *Reconstruction: Studies in Contemporary Culture* 5, no. 4 (Fall 2005). http://reconstruction.eserver.org/054/jowett.shtml.

Kane, Kathryn. "A Very Queer Refusal: The Chilling Effect of the Cullens' Heteronormative Embrace." In Click, Aubrey and Behm-Morawitz, *Bitten by Twilight*, 103–18.

Kelwick, Jamie. Review of *Catwoman*, directed by Pitof, Warner Bros. Pictures. The Usher Speaks, 2004. Accessed July 17, 2005. http://www.kelwick.karoo.net/TheUsher-Speaks2004/TheUsherSpeaks-Catwoman.htm.

Kilgour, Maggie. "Dr. Frankenstein Meets Dr. Freud." In *American Gothic: New Interventions in a National Narrative*, edited by Robert K. Martin and Eric Savoy, 40–53. Iowa City: University of Iowa Press, 1998.

Kisor, Yvette. "Narrative Layering and 'High-Culture' Romance." In Clarke and Osborn, *The Twilight Mystique*, 35–59.

Kokkola, Lydia. "Virtuous Vampires and Voluptuous Vamps: Romance Conventions Reconsidered in Stephenie Meyer's 'Twilight' Series." *Children's Literature in Education* 42, no. 2 (June 2011): 165–79.

La Femme Nikita. Created by Joel Surnow. Produced by Jay Firestone and Jamie Paul Rock. Burbank, CA: Warner Bros. Pictures, 1997–2001. TV.

"The lesson nobody learns." *The Economist*, April 24, 1999, 25-26.

Lippert, Barbara. "Hey There, Warrior Grrrl." *New York*, December 15, 1997.

Livingston, Ira. *Arrow of Chaos: Romanticism and Postmodernity*. Minneapolis: University of Minnesota Press, 1996.

Mack, Robert L. Introduction to *The Castle of Otranto and Hieroglyphic Tales*, by Horace Walpole, xvi–xx. London: Everyman Paperbacks, 1993.

Mann, Thomas. *The Magic Mountain*. Translated by John E. Wood. New York: Alfred A. Knopf, 1995.

Marinucci, Mimi. "Feminism and the Ethics of Violence: Why Buffy Kicks Ass." In *Buffy the Vampire Slayer and Philosophy: Fear and Trembling in Sunnydale*, edited by James B. South, 61–75. Peru, IL: Open Court Publishing, 2003.

Martens, Marianne. "Consumed by Twilight: The Commodification of Young Adult Literature." In Click, Aubrey and Behm-Morawitz, *Bitten by Twilight*, 243–60.

Massé, Michelle A. *In the Name of Love: Women, Masochism, and the Gothic*. Ithaca, New York: Cornell University Press, 1992.

Maturin, Charles. *Melmoth the Wanderer*. Digireads.com Publishing, 2010. digireads.com/ViewBook.aspx?isbn=9781420934946.

McClimans, Leah, and J. Jeremy Wisnewski. "Undead Patriarchy and the Possibility of Love." In Housel and Wisnewski, *Twilight and Philosophy*, 163–75.

McConnell, Kathleen. "Chaos at the Mouth of Hell: Why the Columbine High School Massacre had Repercussions for *Buffy the Vampire Slayer*." *Gothic Studies* 2, no. 1 (April 2000): 119–35.

McDowell, Robin. "Students 'Take Back' Their School: Rally Celebrates Return." *The National Post*, Aug 17, 1999.

Meyer, Stephenie. *Breaking Dawn*. New York: Little, Brown, 2008.

——. *Eclipse*. New York: Little, Brown, 2007.

——. *New Moon*. New York: Little, Brown, 2006.

——. *Twilight*. New York: Little, Brown, 2005.

Morrow, Lance. "Coming to Clarity about Guns." *TIME*, May 3, 1999.

Morse, Donald R. "The Stressful Kiss: A Biopsychosocial Evaluation of the Origins, Evolution and Societal Significance of Vampirism." *Stress Medicine* 9, no. 3 (July 1993): 181–99.

Mulvey, Laura. "Visual Pleasure and Narrative Cinema." *Screen* 16, no. 3 (Autumn 1975): 6–18.

My Fair Lady. Directed by George Cukor. Hollywood: Paramount Pictures, 2009. DVD.

O'Reilly, Julie D. "The Wonder Woman Precedent: Female (Super)Heroism on Trial." *The Journal of American Culture* 28, no. 3 (September 2005): 273–83.

Olson, Tod. "Friends…and Enemies." *Teen People*, August 1999.

Ostow, Micol. "Why I Love Buffy." *Sojourner: The Women's Forum* 24, no. 3 (November 1998): 20.

Ostrow, Joanne. "College life next for 'Buffy.'" *Denver Post*, July 27, 1999. Accessed September 27, 1999. http://extras.denverpost.com/scene/ost0727.htm.

Ovid. "Iphis and Anaxarete." In *Metamorphoses*, 583–87. Translated by David Raeburn. Penguin Classics. London: Penguin, 2004.

———. "Orpheus' Song: Myrrha." In *Metamorphoses*, 396–407. Translated by David Raeburn. Penguin Classics. London: Penguin, 2004.

———. "Orpheus' Song: Pygmalion." In *Metamorphoses*, translated by David Raeburn, 394–96. Penguin Classics. London: Penguin, 2004.

———. "Pygmalion." In *The Metamorphoses of Ovid*. Vol. II, Bk. 10, translated by William Caxton, 15–19. Facsimile Edition. New York: George Braziller, 1968. [No copy of a print edition by Caxton is known.]

———. "Pygmalion." In *Tales from Ovid*, translated by Ted Hughes, 133–39. New York: Farrar, Straus and Giroux, 1997.

———. "The Story of Cinyras and Myrrha." In Ovid's *Metamorphoses in fifteen books*, translated by John Dryden, 329–32. New York: George Macy, 1961.

———. "The Story of Pygmalion and the Statue." In Ovid's *Metamorphoses in fifteen books*, translated by John Dryden, 325–28. New York: George Macy, 1961.

Paglia, Camille. "Sex War: Abortion, Battering, Sexual Harassment." In *Vamps and Tramps: New Essays*, 38–56. New York: Vintage, 1994.

Pender, Patricia. "'Kicking ass is comfort food': Buffy as third wave feminist icon." In *Third Wave Feminism: A Critical Exploration*, edited by Stacy Gillis, Gillian Howie and Rebecca Munford, 175–84. London: Palgrave Macmillan, 2004.

Phillips, Andrew. "Lessons of Littleton." *Maclean's*, May 3, 1999.

Platt, Carrie Anne. "Cullen Family Values: Gender and Sexual Politics in the Twilight Series." In Click, Aubrey and Behm-Morawitz, *Bitten by Twilight*, 71–86.

Pope, Alexander. "Rape of the Lock: An Heroi-Comical Poem." In *Eighteenth Century English Literature*, edited by Geoffrey Tillotson, Marshall Waingrow and Paul Fussell, 567–78. Toronto: Harcourt, Brace & World, 1969.

———. "To a Young Lady, With the Works of Voiture." In *Eighteenth Century English Literature*, edited by Geoffrey Tillotson, Marshall Waingrow and Paul Fussell, 564–65. Toronto: Harcourt, Brace & World, 1969.

Pozner, Jennifer. "Thwack! Pow! Yikes! Not Your Mother's Heroines." *Sojourner: The Women's Forum* 23, no. 2 (October 1997): 12.

Puszczalowski, Philip. "Space, Time, and Vampire Ontology." In Housel and Wisnewski, *Twilight and Philosophy*, 219–26.

"razziechannel." "Halle Berry accepts Razzie Award." The 25th Annual RAZZIE Awards, filmed February 26, 2005. YouTube video, 8:20. Posted January 13, 2011. http://www.youtube.com/watch?v=U-7s_yeQuDg&lr=1.

Regis, Pamela. *A Natural History of the Romance Novel*. Philadelphia: University of Pennsylvania Press, 2007.

Rich, Adrienne. "Resisting Amnesia: History and Personal Life." In *Blood, Bread, and Poetry: Selected Prose 1979–1985*, 136–55. New York: W. W. Norton, 1986.

Ritchie, Anne Thackery. "Mrs. Barbauld." *The Cornhill Magazine* 44 (1881): 599. Accessed July 2010. http://books.google.ca/books?id=CgrSAAAAMA AJ&lpg=PA597&ots=3n8GU5wzEz&dq=mrs.%20barbauld.%20The%20 Cornhill%20Magazine&pg=PA581#v=onepage&q=mrs.%20barbauld.%20 The%20Cornhill%20Magazine&f=false

Rumbold, Valerie. *Women's Place in Pope's World*. New York: Cambridge University Press, 1989.

Samanta, Anamika, and Erin Franzman. "Women in Action." *HUES* 4, no. 3 (Summer 1998): 28–31.

Scheib, Richard. Review of *Catwoman*, directed by Pitof. Moria: The Science Fiction, Horror and Fantasy Film Review. Accessed May 7, 2009. http:// moria.co.nz/fantasy/catwoman-film-2004.htm.

Seifert, Christine. "Bite Me! (Or Don't)" *Bitch Magazine*, 2008. http:// bitchmagazine.org/article/bite-me-or-dont.

Shakespeare, William. *The Winter's Tale*. Edited by Frances E. Dolan. Toronto: Penguin, 1999.

Shaw, George Bernard. Pygmalion. In *The Norton Introduction to English*, 7th ed., edited by Jerome Beaty and J. Paul Hunter, 1414–86. New York: W. W. Norton, 1998.

Shaw, Marc E. "For the Strength of Bella? Meyer, Vampires, and Mormonism." In Housel and Wisnewski, *Twilight and Philosophy*, 227–36.

Sheffield, Jessica, and Elyse Merlo. "Biting Back: Twilight Anti-Fandom and the Rhetoric of Superiority." In Click, Aubrey and Behm-Morawitz, *Bitten by Twilight*, 207–22.

Shelley, Mary Wollstonecraft. *The Journals of Mary Shelley 1814–1844*. Vol. 1. Edited by Paula R. Feldman and Diana Scott-Kilvert. Oxford: The Clarendon Press, 1987.

Shelley, Mary. *Frankenstein, or The Modern Prometheus*. Edited by Johanna M. Smith. Boston, MA: Bedford/St. Martin's, 1992.

Siegel, Carol. "Female Heterosexual Sadism: The Final Feminist Taboo in *Buffy the Vampire Slayer* and the Anita Blake Vampire Hunter Series." In *Third Wave Feminism and Television: Jane Puts it in a Box*, edited by Merri Lisa Johnson, 56–90. New York: I.B.Tauris, 2007.

Snitow, Ann Barr. "Mass Market Romance: Pornography for Women is Different." In *Powers of Desire: The Politics of Sexuality*, edited by Ann Snitow, Christine Stansell and Sharon Thompson, 245–63. New York: Monthly Review Press, 1983.

Stern, Lesley. "Paths That Wind through the Thicket of Things." *Critical Inquiry* 28, no. 1 (Autumn 2001): 317–54.

Tate, Ray. Review of *Catwoman*, directed by Pitof, Warner Bros. Pictures. *Silver Bullet Comic Books* #87. Accessed July 17, 2005.

Taylor, Chris. "Digital Dungeons." *TIME*, May 3, 1999.

Taylor, Chris. "We're Goths and Not Monsters." *TIME*, May 3, 1999.

Tibbetts, John C. "Robots Redux: *A.I. Artificial Intelligence* (2001)." *Literature Film Quarterly* 29, no. 4 (2001): 256–61.

Tillotson, Geoffrey, ed. *The Poems of Alexander Pope*. Vol. 2, *Rape of the Lock and Other Poems*. New Haven, CT: Yale University Press, 1940.

Tjardes, Sue. "'If You're Not Enjoying It, You're Doing Something Wrong': Textual and Viewer Constructions of Faith, the Vampire Slayer." In Early and Kennedy, *Athena's Daughters*, 66–77.

Toscano, Margaret M. "Mormon Morality and Immortality in Stephenie Meyer's Twilight Series." In Click, Aubrey and Behm-Morawitz, *Bitten by Twilight*, 21–36.

True Blood. Created by Alan Ball. Based on the books by Charlaine Harris. New York: HBO, 2008–ongoing. TV.

Tylim, Isaac. "The Vampire Game." *Psychoanalytic Inquiry* 18 no. 2 (1998): 281–90.

Ventura, Michael. "Warrior Women: Why are TV Shows like *Buffy the Vampire Slayer*, *La Femme Nikita*, and *Xena: Warrior Princess* so popular, especially among teens?" *Psychology Today*, November 1998. 58-63.

Veronica Mars. Created by Rob Thomas. Burbank, CA: Warner Bros. Television, 2004–2007. TV.

Wagner, Sally Roesch. "Pornography and the Sexual Revolution: The Backlash of Sadomasochism." In *Against Sadomasochism: A Radical Feminist Analysis*, edited by Robin Ruth Linden, Darlene R. Pagano, Diana E. H. Russell and Susan Leigh Star, 23–44. San Francisco: Frog in the Well, 1982.

Warwick, Alexandra. "Urban Gothic." In *The Handbook to Gothic Literature*, edited by Marie Mulvey-Roberts, 288-89. New York: New York University Press, 1998.

Whedon, Joss. "Angel" interview. *Buffy the Vampire Slayer*, season 1, episode 7. Los Angeles: 20th Century Fox Home Entertainment, 2002. DVD.

——. "Welcome to the Hellmouth" interview. *Buffy the Vampire Slayer*, season 1, episode 1. Los Angeles: 20th Century Fox Home Entertainment, 2002. DVD.

——. "Witch" and "Never Kill a Boy on the First Date" interview. *Buffy the Vampire Slayer*, season 1, episodes 3 and 5. Los Angeles: 20th Century Fox Home Entertainment, 2002. DVD.

Wilson, Natalie. "Civilized Vampires Versus Savage Werewolves: Race and Ethnicity in the Twilight Series." In Click, Aubrey and Behm-Morawitz, *Bitten by Twilight*, 55–70.

Wollstonecraft, Mary. *A Vindication of the Rights of Woman*. Edited by Carol H. Poston. Norton Critical Editions. New York: W. W. Norton, 1975.

Xena: Warrior Princess. Created by John Schulian, Robert G. Tapert. Beverly Hills, CA: Anchor Bay Entertainment, 1995–2001. TV.

Žižek, Slavoj. *Welcome to the Desert of the Real!: Five Essays on September 11 and Related Dates*. New York: Verso, 2002.

INDEX

Published under the pen name Kathy Mac, Kathleen McConnell's *Nail Builders Plan for Strength and Growth* (2002) won the Lampert Award for best first book of poems in Canada, and was a finalist for the Governor General's Award. *The Hundefräulein Papers* (2009) chronicles the years she spent living with, and looking after the dogs of Elisabeth Mann Borgese. After a typically peripatetic writer's life, she has settled in Fredericton, New Brunswick, where she teaches Creative Writing and Women Writers in the English Department at St. Thomas University.